WHO THEY ARE

AND WHAT THEY'RE UP TO

WHO THEY ARE

AND WHAT THEY'RE UP TO

LESLIE AND STEPHEN SHAW

TRAVELING SHOES PRESS
PO BOX 332
Pioneertown, CA 92268

Who They Are | And What They're Up To
ISBN# 979-8-218-09742-4

© 2022 Leslie and Stephen Shaw

Book design by Jon Christopher

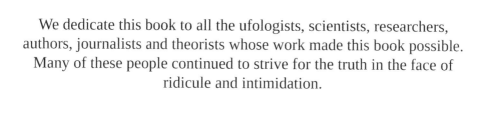

We dedicate this book to all the ufologists, scientists, researchers, authors, journalists and theorists whose work made this book possible. Many of these people continued to strive for the truth in the face of ridicule and intimidation.

PREFACE

Human beings can be divided into two groups; those who have seen UFOs and those who have not.

Once you see one, you can't unsee it, you can't go back to a place of happy ignorance, where you can believe everyone who has seen a UFO is a crazy nutball.

Those who have seen them all have the same questions: What are they? Who is flying them? Where did they come from and why are they here? In this book we will be attempting to answer these questions.

My husband and I have had several bizarre experiences that have been the inspiration for this book. I am a semi-retired journalist, so I have done almost all the writing and my husband Stephen has been my fellow theorist, researcher and soundboard. We have both had a lifelong interest in the subject of UFOs and are both well read in the genre. My husband was present for both of my bizarre experiences, so we'll start there.

We had been to a meeting of our art club on a winter evening in 2005. We were driving west on Highway 62 in Joshua Tree, California, heading to our Yucca Valley home, when we saw a bright, round, white light straight ahead of us. At first I thought it was a plane flying into the Palm Springs airport, but it didn't have the other lights you would expect to see on a plane. It got brighter and brighter as if it were coming toward us. Suddenly, the light streaked away to the north and was gone over the northern horizon in about a quarter of a second. It immediately went full speed at what must have been thousands of miles per hour.

There is no known aircraft that can do that, and no human pilot could survive that kind of acceleration.

Our second joint sighting was in October of 2020 in our backyard in Desert Hot Springs, also in California. In the night sky we saw another round, white light. It was moving in a way that no aircraft can move. It was zipping around at various speeds but mostly very fast, changing direction with no change in velocity. It stopped and hovered for a few seconds, then shot off at another angle, doing this kind of maneuver several times. It did not slow down to stop, but instantly stopped; it did not slowly accelerate to full speed, but went from a dead stop to full speed instantly. It was not performing banked turns like any kind of plane would. Then it sped away to the north again at an incredible speed.

My husband and his family had years of strange experiences. The following is Stephen telling his story.

I'll start with some familial background. My mother's side of the family had a history of practicing automatic writing, table levitating and contact with spirit guides back to my great-grandparents (at least). Both my parents were born in the north of England just prior to World War II. I was born in the USA. My education and world experience spans music, military duty, woodworking and construction, studying and teaching Tai Chi Chuan since the age of 17 and working as a practitioner of Chinese medicine and acupuncture for over twenty years.

I can recall my first unusual memories from the age of three happening at our Woodland Hills, California, home. I would commonly be awakened in my bed by an invisible being jumping on my chest and stomach. It was not malevolent; just playful.

The second strange incident happened when I was about nine years old. I know because of the bunk bed I was just then sleeping in. I heard rustling in the living room and climbed out of the top bunk and proceeded to walk very slowly and quietly down the dark hallway to the living room, heart pounding fearfully. The next thing I remember was being back in bed sometime later with no memory at all of what had happened. I have tried many times to unblock the memory of the incident to no effect.

The next group of major events, also in Woodland Hills, occurred when I was 18 and they were experienced by my father, sister and me over a one week period in January of 1978. The first night all three of us heard the sound of a silver bell being rung repeatedly inside the wall next to the fireplace. The odd thing about this was that I had just been reading *Metaphysical Meditations* by Paramahansa Yogananda and gave the booklet to my dad to peruse. Not more than ten minutes later (at approximately 9 p.m.), my dad came into my room with a puzzled expression and said, "I must be hearing things. Can you come into the living room, Stephen?" My dad was a master cabinet maker and knew that bells don't ring inside a two-by-four-inch wall. Sure enough, there was a repeating, resonant ring. I got my sister and she heard it, too. We banged on the wall, looked up the chimney and just felt perplexed. After about ten minutes, it stopped.

The next night, my dad's closet doors opened and closed by themselves. This spooked him a bit.

The following night, I was lying on the bottom bunk in my room, when I was awakened by a strange "whizzing" sound. My bedroom door was open and I turned over in bed to look down the hall to try to figure out where the sound was coming from. I rolled over and tried to go back to sleep, when my bed started to shake. It felt like someone was pushing from the foot of the bed. I thought for a moment it was my own movements, and I tried to relax, but it happened again. The motion was even stronger the second time and stronger again the third time. Each push came in two distinct shoves. At this point, my adrenaline was making my heart race. Then I felt three distinct taps on my right shoulder. It felt like a tap from a single index finger. I quickly rolled over expecting to see something and I shouted, "What!" but there was nothing there, although

I could still feel a presence. I then blacked out and have no memory of what happened next.

The next night, I decided to sleep in my work clothes of the day on the living room couch. I awoke around 5 a.m. It was still dark and I noticed the sound of the fountain in the extra room; then I looked at my piano. I was awake and not dreaming. The next thing that happened was both fantastic and scary. A being of blue-white light came from the front door, which faced east directly behind my head. The being seemed to walk (or somehow move) quickly toward me. The entire room was filled with a blue-white light. The being stopped at my right side by my right ear, and then the entire right side of my body became numb and was immobilized. I experienced a fifty-fifty mix of excitement and fear. I believed this might be the family spirit guide, Ole Glegly, that I had heard about since I was a child. The being bent down and clearly said into my ear, "Hi, Steve," in a friendly whisper. A few seconds later, the being reversed direction and left the house. My numbness faded and I woke my dad.

Later that day, at 11:30 a.m., I decided to buy some breakfast for my dad and me, and I reached into the right pocket of the work clothes I was still wearing from the day before. I found that all the coins and nails that were in my pocket when the being had paralyzed me were magnetized! I could pick up the coins and the nails all sticking to each other. My dad saw it too. We didn't know what to think.

A day or two later, my dad woke up in the middle of the night, and looked out his bedroom door down the hall into my room. My door was open and he could see that my bedroom was completely filled with a blue-white light. A voice told him telepathically, "Relax, Geoffrey, go back to sleep. Everything is fine." My dad fell back to sleep.

A few years later, at the age of 23, while living in the same house, I was lying on the floor in the living room about 4:30 a.m. There was a light on in the room and I looked up to see a small being, about two-and-a-half-feet tall, floating next to one of the ceiling beams. It was all black with a triangular head, squarish feet and big black eyes. As soon as it realized I was looking at it, it floated down to my right side, and spoke to me in a deep baritone voice saying, "Do you want me to help you get out of your body?" I felt a deep, tingling sense of fear in my gut, but my instincts told me not to show any fear. I responded, "You can help me, but you cannot possess me." I still don't know why I said that. The being grabbed my arm and started to pull me, but I resisted and I didn't come out of my body. The being then made a wailing growl of frustration, rose back up to the ceiling and faded away.

Further history and related events that I have experienced include hundreds of occasions of distinct knocking sounds on the wall behind my head just as I am trying to sleep. Always three knocks. I regularly experience uncontrollable astral projecting and something I call "the astral hurricane," which is just what it sounds like; my astral body is blown out of my body or sometimes spins inside my body.

During the years that Leslie and I studied chakra opening, meditation and astral projection techniques, we started projecting almost immediately. For me it was more of a re-learning than anything, yet our experiences were radically different. For Leslie, the experience of directed projection was fun and positive. For me, it was scary.

Also, my lucid dreams became terrifying. One time, Leslie went to make coffee and returned as a giant snake that attacked me. The real Leslie came into the room right in the middle of the snake biting me. Another time, I traveled to the moon and tried to escape from an alien by hiding in a coffin. I was sexually assaulted in a horrible way that time. I felt that these astral projection practices were too frightening for me and I gave them up.

I must also say that these experiences for my family members and me were never drug-induced and they spanned at least three generations. My now dead uncle on my mother's sister's side (not a direct blood relation, but married to my aunt) had experiences of missing time and unexplained visitations.

My brother built a home for himself in a remote forest location. He started experiencing visitations from a small, silver sphere that floated up and down his deck. One time this sphere rushed him and flew straight through his neck. The next day he had bruising on his upper back where the sphere must have exited.

All his other incidents happened in his youth at the family home in Sonora, California. One night he saw two white, round UFOs outside his window.

Another time he saw a tall, skinny, silvery-gray being outside his bedroom door right before he blacked out.

Another night he heard what he thought was a cat scrabbling under his bed. When he reached down, a hand grabbed his arm and again he blacked out.

Later we learned that he also suffered from missing time periods.

He had many health problems throughout his life, suffered from anxiety and in 2017 ended his life in a horrible murder suicide where he killed our mother and himself with a shotgun. My wife and I both believe his mental health was affected by these strange, otherworldly experiences and possibly facilitated his horrible end.

CONTENTS

CHAPTER ONE

HISTORY OF UFO ACTIVITY, MOSTLY IN THE UNITED STATES

Yes, UFOs are real. Anyone who has seen a UFO, or believes others who have seen them, has asked themself these questions: who are they, where do they come from and what are they doing here? Are these alien spaceships or is there another explanation?

In this book we will endeavor to answer these questions.

Some questions concerning UFOs were answered in a National Security Agency report,

"UFO Hypothesis and Survival Questions" (1968), released by a Freedom of Information Act request.

"The fact that UFO phenomena have been witnessed all over the world from ancient times, and by considerable numbers of reputable scientists in recent times, indicates rather strongly that UFOs are not all hoaxes. Rather than diminishing, if anything, the modern trend is toward increased reports from all sources." [1]

Another question we should be asking ourselves is why are there so many sightings? Worldwide there are over 10,000 sightings per year.

UFOs commonly have three different acronyms: UFOs, obviously, (unidentified flying objects), UAPs (unidentified aerial phenomena) and USOs (unidentified submerged objects), and ufologists have been tracking and counting their associated activities for many years. Sightings of these objects number in the hundreds of thousands if not millions.

UFO sightings have been taking place for hundreds, if not thousands of years. According to the National UFO Reporting Center, in the forty-seven years of its existence, there have been over 150,000 reports in the US alone, an average of about 3,200 a year, jumping to six thousand in 2019. Presumably, reported incidents are only a fraction of the number of actual sightings. [2]

They are frequently reported by reputable witnesses, tracked on military and commercial radar and have left measurable effects on places where they have landed, such as crushed vegetation and residual radiation signatures.

This is not a fringe phenomena witnessed by a handful of lunatics; it is a persistent, worldwide constant.

Another good question we will be addressing in this book is why did the US government, and other governments of the world, work so hard to cover up UFO activity?

Except for the first two chapters, this book will not spend much time convincing the reader to believe in UFOs. It will instead presume that they are a well-established fact seen and photographed by hundreds of thousands of witnesses. It will also assume as fact that the beings flying around in UFOs are abducting people and performing experiments on them and that these beings have a far superior technology to our own.

The following summations are to briefly catch the layman reader up to what is known about UFO activity in the US.

UFOs seem to be particularly interested in military bases and the military activities of several nations, but especially those of the US.

During World War II, US fighter pilots reported glowing orbs flying around their planes in the battles over Germany. These sightings were a regular occurrence and hundreds of cases were reported.

These orbs were eventually dubbed "foo fighters." Pilots were unable to explain their existence and many believed they were some kind of Nazi secret weapon.

Some pilots reported their engines cutting out when the foo fighters were near, and they were able to reignite them after the orbs left.

German pilots were also seeing them, and also thinking they were a secret weapon of their enemies. [3]

Following the end of World War II and the US' use of nuclear weapons at Hiroshima and Nagasaki, UFO sightings drastically increased. The UFOs seemed to have a particular interest in military bases conducting nuclear testing or research.

Everyone has heard about the famous Roswell crash incident, but most people don't realize that during the decade following the end of World War II, there were many flying saucer crashes in the US and other countries. [4]

We know a UFO crash took place April 12, 1941, in Cape Girardeau, Missouri. At this site there were the bodies of three dead Grey aliens. The incident is known as *M0-41: The Bombshell Before Roswell.* The military quickly took charge of the site and flew the bodies and the craft to Washington, D.C. This was supposedly the first time our military had access to alien technology. [5][23]

There were two very significant UFO incidents between the time of the Cape Girardeau and Roswell crashes.

THE LOS ANGELES INCIDENT

There was a mass UFO sighting in the city of Los Angeles around 3 a.m. on February 25, 1942. A silver, oval-shaped UFO was seen hovering over the ocean just off the coast of Hermosa Beach. [6]

This happened about two months after the Japanese had attacked Pearl Harbor, plunging the US into World War II. The population of the US and its military were very jumpy, worried about further threats to the Pacific Coast by Japanese forces. So it's not surprising that the Coast

Guard began firing anti-aircraft shells at the object. The 37th Coast Artillery Brigade bombarded the object and woke up millions of civilians who rushed out to see what was happening. Roughly 1,400 anti-aircraft shells were fired.

Witnesses claimed the object moved away to the south and a flight of US military fighter planes streaked across the sky after it. This fighter response was never admitted to by the military.

The UFO was seen by about one million people and was possibly the largest UFO sighting in history.

At first the Navy attributed the incident to war nerves, but Secretary of War Henry Stimson took offense to the accusation and defended the military men's actions, saying they were firing on an actual craft. [6]

OPERATION HIGHJUMP

We know that Rear Admiral Richard E. Byrd, a famous American naval officer and explorer, led a military expedition called Operation Highjump to the South Pole in early 1947. Sources indicate the men in the operation fought a battle with flying saucers that emerged from the water, sank a destroyer and shot down about half of Byrd's carrier-based aircraft. Read more about this incident in Chapter 3. [7]

THE ROSWELL INCIDENT

The now famous Roswell crash took place on July 3, 1947. A UFO crashed on a ranch, owned by Mac Brazel, outside Roswell, New Mexico. The UFO crashed into a hill and broke in two, with a large piece flying farther forward, leaving two crash sites. [4 8 9 10]

Brazel found a debris field and what appeared to be alien bodies. The aliens were described as being three to four feet tall, with oversized heads, three to five fingers, black, wrap-around eyes, slits for mouths and long arms – what ufologists have come to call the Greys.

The nearby Roswell Army Airfield scrambled to the scene and collected all the evidence of the crash.

A local mortician, Glenn Dennis, claimed the Roswell base ordered several child-sized coffins from him right after the crash.

Brazel reported finding what appeared to be tin foil, but said it must have been some kind of "memory metal" because when he crumpled it up, it would re-flatten by itself.

The crash was followed by a media sensation when the incident was reported in the Roswell Daily Record newspaper with the headline, "RAAF Captures Flying Saucer on Ranch in Roswell Region."

A government coverup took place immediately after, and the next day's headline retracted the first story and said a weather balloon had crashed.

Witnesses to the crash site and the alien bodies were threatened with the murder of themselves and their family members and ordered to keep silent about what they'd seen.

UFO investigator Don Schmitt collected enough deathbed confessions from witnesses to produce a documentary film on the subject called *Roswell UFO Crash: Deathbed Confessions.*

The remains of the wreckage and the bodies were eventually studied at Area 51. The government denied the existence of the base until they admitted it was real in 2013. This base was supposedly set up to handle any future extraterrestrial technology that came into the government's possession for the purposes of reverse engineering the tech. [24]

Walter Haut was the public relations officer at the Roswell Army Air Field and he was the officer who wrote the initial Roswell press release that had caused the sensation. The Disclosure Project, a nonprofit founded by Steven Greer in 1993 to find out the truth about UFO activity, obtained Haut's "deathbed confession" about the press release. Haut claimed the news that the military had in its possession an alien flying saucer was "given to me almost verbatim by Colonel Blanchard."

Haut claimed to have seen much of the debris from the crash. He said he was able to touch the material and that he was able to crumple in his hand a piece of metal that would then go back to its original form, confirming what Brazel had said. According to Haut, this was not technology that was manmade. He also said he saw the entities from the crash, describing them as having larger than normal heads and looking like 10-year-old children, which ties into the testimony of the mortician. [11]

THE ALIEN AUTOPSIES

We believe alien autopsies were performed on the victims of the Roswell UFO crash.

An alien autopsy film, *Alien Autopsy: Fact or Fiction,* was released to the world in 1995 by a producer named Ray Santilli who claimed he purchased the film from an aging military cameraman. [12]

The film's producer has made conflicting statements concerning the authenticity of the footage in the show over the years, but in the spring of 2021, he put a single frame of what he claims is the original footage up for auction for one million dollars, opening himself up to a hefty lawsuit if the frame should be found to be fake. [12]

Whether Santilii's film is a complete hoax or not, evidence that these autopsies were performed is supported by the testimony of Army Colonel Philip J. Corso, who recorded a confession with the Disclosure Project and wrote a book, *The Day After Roswell*, in which he claimed that while he was a major working as the on-duty officer at Fort Riley, Kansas, he opened a crate containing a dead alien body floating in a fluid. This took place a few days after the Roswell crash. When he asked where it came from, he was told an airfield in New Mexico.

He also said that in 1961 when he was a colonel working for National Security at the White House during the Eisenhower administration, he read reports on alien autopsies from the 1947 Roswell crash. According to Corso, the autopsies were performed in a special military lab at Walter Reed Hospital. At this time, Corso's job at the White House was to slowly feed alien technology into the research and development departments of US private sector corporations. [11]

THE GOVERNMENT BASES AND PROGRAMS

In May of 1989, a physicist named Bob Lazar claimed he worked at a section of the Area 51 base called S4, an even more secret part of an already highly sensitive, secret base. In a series of public interviews done by George Knapp, Lazar spoke about his work reverse engineering nine flying saucer spacecraft stored at S4. Lazar claimed that before working at S4, he was a physicist at Los Alamos National Laboratory, the facility that created the nuclear bomb. Knapp was able to confirm that he'd worked there. Knapp researched Lazar's claims and found him credible. Witnesses have come forward to attest to the existence of the S4 area and have confirmed Lazar had worked there. [13] [24]

Just three weeks after Roswell, President Truman signed the National Security Act of 1947, which created the National Security Council and the Central Intelligence Agency. This policy of national security was called the National Security State and is said to have been the start of the Cold War.

We know a top secret, three-page letter was sent from US Air Force Lt. General Nathan F. Twining, the commanding general of the Air Materiel Command at Wright-Patterson Air Force Base, to the commanding general of the Army Air Forces in Washington, D.C., Brigadier General

George Schulgen on September 23, 1947. The subject line was, "AMC Opinion Concerning 'Flying Discs.'" [14]

This document is now called the Twining Memorandum, and ufologists consider it to be one of the most important UFO documents of that decade. Twining's opinion was formed after conferring with personnel from technology, engineering and intelligence officers. In it Twining wrote, "The phenomenon is something real and not visionary or fictitious. There are objects probably approximating the shape of a disc, of such appreciable size as to appear to be as large as man-made aircraft…, The reported operating characteristics such as extreme rates of climb, maneuverability (particularly in roll), and motion which must be considered evasive when sighted or contacted by friendly aircraft and radar, lend belief to the possibility that some of the objects are controlled either manually, automatically or remotely."

He described UFOs as "metallic or light reflecting surfaces. Absence of trail, except in a few instances where the object apparently was operating under high performance conditions. Circular or elliptical in shape, flat on bottom and domed on top. Several reports of well-kept formation flights varying from three to nine objects. Normally no associated sound, except in three instances a substantial rumbling roar was noted. Level flight speeds normally above three hundred knots are estimated."

"Due consideration must be given [to] … the possibility that some foreign nation has a form of propulsion, possibly nuclear, which is outside of our domestic knowledge."

The general recommended that, "Headquarters, Army Air Forces issue a directive assigning a priority, security classification and code name for a detailed study of this matter to include the preparation of complete sets of all available and pertinent data."

The next day, on September 24, 1947, two months after the Roswell incident, Truman created a top secret committee of military and scientific specialists, called the Majestic 12, also called MJ-12 or Majic-12. These experts created a restricted UFO response operations manual, SOM1-

WARNING! This is a TOP SECRET—MAJIC EYES ONLY document containing compartmentalized information essential to the national security of the United States. EYES ONLY ACCESS to the material herein is strictly limited to personnel possessing MAJIC—12 CLEARANCE LEVEL. Examination or use by unauthorized personnel is strictly forbidden and is punishable by federal law

MAJESTIC—12 GROUP   •   APRIL 1954

01, entitled "Extraterrestrial Entities and Technology Recovery and Disposal," labeled as "top secret/MAJIC EYES ONLY." It outlined the committee's official secrecy policy adopted in April of 1954. This controversial document was anonymously leaked to a UFO researcher.

We know that UFO activities were later referred to as Operation Majestic Twelve and this information was limited to the office of the president, the MJ-12 committee and the director of Central Intelligence. [15]

We know that on December 11, 1952, these experts created Project Blue Book, ostensibly created to further study UFO phenomena, but really designed to explain the incidents away. This committee was mandated with not only studying UFO activity but also setting policy on how to treat the phenomena in the public and the media. [4 15 16 17 18 19]

We know these policies were to cover up these incidents to the public, while at the same time gathering all pertinent information for themselves.

Under Project Blue Book, the government enacted a policy of lying to the public about what they already knew of UFO activity and anything they subsequently learned.

We know the government cover-up policy first utilized public ridicule to humiliate witnesses into silence. If this failed, they would use threats against witnesses and their families, and if this failed they would use retaliatory methods such as forcing witnesses out of their jobs and ruining their reputations and careers. Though not actually sanctioned in the manual, we believe that in extreme cases, Project Blue Book operatives would resort to murder. Yes, murders, most of which were explained away as suicides.

One such possible murder was the suspicious death of one of the Majestic-12 members, former Secretary of Defense James Forrestal, on May 22, 1949. Forrestal supposedly jumped to his death out of a sixteenth-floor window of the Bethesda Medical Center in Bethesda, Maryland. This death was ruled to be a suicide, but it is believed by UFO researchers that Forrestal wanted to be more transparent with the public and he was killed to silence him.

There were several suspicious aspects to his death. Supposedly he became severely depressed after his removal from office. He was flown to Florida where his wife was vacationing and was diagnosed by Dr. William Menninger. Rather than being admitted to the doctor's clinic, a facility well qualified to handle his condition, he was instead flown to Bethesda.

According to Dolan's book *UFOs and the National Security State: Chronology of a Cover-Up, 1941 to 1973,* Forrestal was "committed to the VIP suite of the National Naval Medical Center, an odd destination considering that Forrestal was no longer a government employee."

Forrestal's brother confirmed that access to him became severely limited, and when he tried to have his brother discharged, the suicide followed. He was last seen at 1:45 a.m. when he refused a sedative because he wanted to continue copying a passage from a play. He was dead fifteen minutes later. He supposedly jumped out of his bathroom window, though the window in the room where he was working was much larger. [4]

According to Dolan, "…he had the belt to his bathrobe tied around his throat, but there was no evidence that it had been tied to anything inside the bathroom, as he would have done if attempting to hang himself."

Why would a man considered a possible suicide risk be placed in a room on the sixteenth floor?

His death was immediately ruled a suicide before any investigation could be conducted and no police inquiry was permitted.

Dolan pointed out other strange occurrences connected to the death: "...(T)he day that Forrestal stepped down … Secretary of the Air Force Stuart Symington, no friend of Forrestal's, told him that he needed to speak to Forrestal confidentially. They rode back to the Pentagon in the same vehicle. Witnesses say that whatever the pair discussed, it had a traumatic impact on Forrestal, who very nearly entered a catatonic state."

Forrestal was in a position to know a great deal about the UFO phenomenon. According to Dolan, Forrestal kept a diary that was immediately seized by the Truman administration.

Whether you believe the Project Blue Book manual to be authentic or not, or if you believe the death of Forrestal to be murder or suicide, there is no doubt the tactics described in the manual became the enacted policy of Project Blue Book.

If you have ever listened to a person's UFO account and laughed at them, you have been influenced by Project Blue Book's use of ridicule. The making of UFO sightings into a big joke was perpetrated by this project.

MORE UFO CRASHES

We know there was another UFO crash six years after the Roswell incident in Arizona, but this time the government had learned from their mistakes at Roswell and completed the cover up so quickly and successfully that the knowledge of the crash was suppressed until the 1970s.

This incident happened on May 21, 1953. A flying saucer crashed into a hill about eight miles north east of Kingman, Arizona. The military successfully cordoned off the area, but scientific experts were brought in to examine the saucer; afterward they were all forced to sign non-disclosure agreements. One of these scientists later came forward with the information, spurring other disclosures as well. [20][21][22][23]

As mentioned above, though the Roswell crash is the most famous, it is not the only UFO crash to take place in the US. Several other crashes are known to have occurred, but the cover-up procedure was handled more efficiently and the news was not leaked to the press in the same way the Roswell incident had been.

OTHER REPORTED UFO CRASH INCIDENTS IN THE US INCLUDE:

Cadotte Pass, Missouri, in September of 1864. A Rocky Mountain trapper, James Lumley, reported an incident to the Cincinnati Commercial newspaper in October of 1865. He told a story of seeing a bursting of a sky rocket while on a trapping trip. It was followed by a fierce wind that ended just as abruptly. The next day he found a path cut through the trees. He followed the devastation to what he at first thought was a stone driven into a hill. Upon closer inspection the stone was filled with compartments and had hieroglyphics written on it. [23]

Benkelman, Nebraska, in June of 1884. Some cowboys from Dundy County reported finding a cylindrical object that crashed on the prairie and left bits of machinery glowing from the heat. [23][31]

Burlington, Vermont, on July 3, 1907. This is probably a near-crash incident. Townspeople saw a ball of fire descending and exploding above a street in the town. The blast knocked over a horse. One witness claimed to have seen part of the descent, the blast that knocked over the horse and then saw the object shoot up into the sky. [23]

San Antonio, New Mexico, in August of 1945. Witnesses saw the US Army removing an avocado-shaped ship from a crash site in the desert. [24] [26]

Corona, New Mexico, also in July of 1947. Writer Don Berliner and nuclear physicist Stanton Friedman investigated this incident and wrote a book about the crash and the US government cover up called, *Crash at Corona: The U.S. Military Retrieval and Cover-Up of a UFO*. [27]

Hopi Reservation, Arizona, on August 13, 1947. Six Native Americans discovered a still-smoldering metallic object crashed in the New Mexico desert. Inside they found an alien creature who, though injured, was still alive. Hearing the approach of military troops, the men decided to keep the being from capture and care for him themselves. Taking him to their home, they found the being could communicate with them through a crystal device that conveyed images. [23] [29]

Cave Creek, and Paradise Valley, Arizona, October 2, 1947. Fox 10 news reported on rumors and Frank Scully wrote a book called *Behind the Flying Saucers* about the incident. In the book, Scully said that in October of 1947 an alien space saucer crashed in the valley. It bounced, skipped and landed miles away in Cave Creek or Paradise Valley. [33]

Aztec, New Mexico, in February of 1948. Three radar units tracked a falling UFO. Secretary of State George C. Marshall requested a search party be dispatched from Camp Hale in Colorado. A helicopter team found a crashed thirty-foot disc twelve miles northeast of Aztec and recovered between two and twelve badly burned humanoids. The disc was stored in Hangar 18 at Wright-Patterson AFB near Dayton, Ohio. [23] [29] [30]

South of Laredo, Texas, in August of 1948. A book was written about this incident called *Fallen Angel: UFO Crash Near Laredo, Texas* by Noe Torres. US military aircraft chased a fast-moving, ninety-foot-diameter silver disc across Texas before watching it crash about thirty miles south-southwest of Laredo. A military retrieval team reportedly recovered the UFO and the body of its non-human occupant from the impact site. Torres appeared on several programs and he became a director of the Mutual UFO Network (MUFON) in South Texas. [23][28]

Hebgen Lake, Montana, August of 1949. A US Air Force document of August 1949 details the reported crash of two UFOs at Hebgen Lake. Seven saucers were seen. [24][38]

Death Valley, California, also in August of 1949. Two prospectors named Mace Garney and Buck Fitzgerald claimed to have watched an object crash (or land) in the desert. It was a twenty-four-foot disc. Two dwarfs emerged but were lost in the sand dunes when pursued. The object disappeared. The story appeared in the local Bakersfield newspaper the next day. [23][29]

Birmingham, Alabama, in mid 1950. When a disc crashed near Birmingham, the area was cordoned off and humanoid bodies were flown to Maxwell Air Force Base, according to a man who claims to have flown the helicopter with the bodies to a waiting aircraft. [23][30]

Ely, Nevada, August 14, 1952. A disc was said to have crashed near Ely, Nevada, and sixteen bodies were allegedly recovered. [23]

Braxton County, West Virginia, in September of 1952. A woman and six boys saw what they described as a "monster." The sighting coincided with a wave of UFO reports, some of which described a possible crash. At least one eyewitness said the monster appeared to be mechanical in nature, a structured machine of some type, rather than a flesh-and-blood creature. [24][32]

New Paltz, New York, in March of 1960. Local law enforcement authorities allegedly captured a small humanoid outside his craft while two copilots escaped. The alien was turned over to the CIA and died twenty-eight days later. [23]

Fort Riley Army Base, Kansas, December 10, 1964. A guard on duty in the motor pool and three other men were ordered by a senior officer to make their way to a remote corner of the base where they saw a military chopper shining a searchlight on a strange object resting on the ground. The guard described the object as "like a giant hamburger." He said the air near the craft was very warm despite it being a bitterly cold night. Other sources claimed nine alien bodies were recovered. [23]

Kecksburg, Pennsylvania, December 9, 1965. This is a very famous case with hundreds of witnesses in Michigan, Ohio and Pennsylvania, who observed a UFO crash. The object's total visible journey lasted no more than six minutes, which indicated a speed far too slow for a meteor and it appeared to change direction. A witness calculated a speed of only around 1,000 miles per hour. Pilots spoke of being buffeted by shockwaves as the object sped by. Several bits of silvery debris were found on the ground at Lapeer, Michigan. It came to rest in a wooded area near Kecksburg. A woman reported the crash and then went to investigate. She found that a military unit had beaten her to the crash site. They took command and told all civilians, police and fire department officials to leave the site immediately. The military unit reported to the police that they had found nothing. UFO investigators found out that the fire service had come within two hundred feet of the object before being turned away. They reported seeing blue flashing lights, and noticed that the tops of several of the trees nearby were broken as if an object had come crashing through. [23 25]

Chili, New Mexico, on May 17, 1974. An Air Force team allegedly removed a sixty-foot-wide metallic object from an impact area and moved it to Kirtland Air Force Base. [29 30]

Council Bluffs, Iowa, in December of 1977. Three young people saw a reddish object about five hundred to six hundred feet in the air falling straight down. It disappeared behind the trees of Big Lake Park followed by a flash of bluish-white light and two "arms of fire" shooting over ten feet in the air suggesting an impact. The three drove to the park and saw a glowing, orange blob with a bluish crystalline substance in its center on a dike about sixteen feet from the road. One of them said it "looked like a great big sparkler." Lava-like material was running down the dike appearing to slow as it cooled. It was too hot to touch and ignited a small grass fire. [35]

Niagara Falls, New York, on April 15, 1992. A large disc-shaped craft was observed coming out of the lake and flew erratically south towards Lockport, New York. The object appeared to be in trouble. When the UFO crashed it managed to avoid hitting the cars traveling the road. The UFO was a hundred feet in diameter and twenty-five feet high. Military, firemen and the police quickly arrived and cleaned up the crash site and cautioned witnesses not to talk about the incident. [23]

Long Island, New York, on November 24, 1992. The Long Island UFO Network (LIUFON) investigated this crash and acquired video and photographs. A poor-quality video showed people examining a bright, reddish, metallic object about four feet square, emitting a white, cloudy gas. A person is seen trying to lift what appears to be a body. Uniformed men arrived and covered the object with a shiny cover. Witnesses reported weird lights and a loud rumbling, and a fire resulted from the crash. Some residents reported strange power surges. Authorities immediately closed off the area for three days and military helicopters flew over the area for days after. When LIUFON later gained admittance to the area, they found a burned area, bent trees and a higher-than-normal radiation reading. [23]

Needles, California, on May 14, 2008. A large object with a turquoise hue plummeted out of the sky and plowed into the earth south of Las Vegas. Eyewitnesses say this was no meteorite, especially since a bunch of helicopters hauled it away. An ex-police-chief Frank Costigan was a witness. [29] [36]

Oahu, Hawaii, in January of 2021. Thousands were mesmerized by a mysterious flurry of lights that appeared to float across Hawaii's evening sky. Photos and videos of the string of lights flooded social media, leaving many to believe the sighting could be anything from a spaceship carrying extra terrestrials to a meteor shower. [37]

A famous UFO incident was involved in another crash, but it wasn't the UFO that crashed this time. Captain Thomas F. Mantell, a P-51 Mustang fighter pilot, crashed his plane in pursuit of a UFO on January 17, 1948. This event was highly publicized at the time. [39]

We know there have been similar crashes in other countries, including Russia, China, Canada, Colombia, Argentina, Brazil, Australia, Italy, Chile, Belgium, Pakistan, Germany, Poland, Guatemala, Sweden, Norway, Denmark, Mexico, South Africa, Slovenia, Cyprus, Kazakhstan, Bolivia, Lebanon, Greece and the UK. Russia and the UK are also supposedly trying to reverse engineer the alien technology.

THE ALIENS WON'T BE IGNORED

Admiral Byrd is believed to have written a diary near the end of his life describing an alien encounter he and his flight crew experienced during a flight over the North Pole on February 19, 1947, while Byrd was supposedly leading Operation Highjump at the South Pole. We believe this meeting really did take place, but for whatever reason, Byrd changed the reported location from the South Pole to the North Pole. [40]

During the flight his plane was forced to land and he was met by Nordic-looking aliens. In an audience with one of them, he was warned about the use of nuclear weapons and told to give the message to his leaders.

During this meeting the alien told Byrd that they had tried to contact us in the past, but their craft had been fired upon. We believe he may have been referring to the Los Angeles incident.

We'll talk more about this meeting in Chapter 3.

When President Truman apparently ignored the Nordic aliens' warning, they took action to force the government into negotiations. Over two weekends starting on July 19, 1952, multiple flying saucers buzzed the

Washington D.C. Capitol and White House complex. The Washington National Airport picked up seven objects on their radar near Andrews Air Force Base. When they were first detected they were moving at about 130 miles per hour, but then the objects accelerated and vanished off the radar moving at about 7,000 miles per hour. They were also picked up by the Andrews radar. [4 16 41 42]

For the next six hours between eight and ten UFOs were tracked. Several pilots also saw the objects as orange lights. Interceptors were scrambled but by the time they arrived, the objects were gone.

Over the following week Washington D.C. continued to be plagued by UFO activity.

On July 26, the objects returned to the Capitol and were again tracked on radar and seen by aviators. As interceptors arrived the objects vanished.

We believe secret communications began between the government and the Nordic aliens after these incidents.

UFO reports had increased in the months before and after the Capitol incident. Project Blue Book received seventy-nine reports in May and 149 reports in June. The Air Force Technical Intelligence Center (ATIC) received 536 reports in July. Most of the reports were coming from military personnel and pilots. The entities behind the UFO activity were apparently demanding the attention of the government.

On July 28, Project Blue Book received fifty UFO reports in one day. On July 29, the Air Force held a press conference and claimed the Washington incidents were caused by "weather phenomena."

Sometimes fighter jets were deployed to intercept and engage the UFOs, but they would just speed away at supersonic speeds; once clocked at 12,000 miles per hour.

During this summer, UFO activity also increased over Europe and Africa.

After the Washington incident, the CIAs Office of Scientific Intelligence's special UFO study group, with the agreement of the Air Force, tightened security on any interactions with the press and the public. [4]

We know that Truman and the MJ-12 advised incoming President Eisenhower to continue the secrecy policy in regards to UFOs.

An eight-page memo was sent from Admiral Roscoe Hillenkoetter, the first director of the CIA and the leader of the Majestic-12 group, to President-Elect Dwight Eisenhower that briefed him on MJ-12 operations and recommended he continue the government's policy of secrecy in relation to UFO information. [16]

President Truman signed the National Security Council Directive 6, establishing the National Security Agency on October 24, 1952, uniting all military intelligence operations under its umbrella. The NSA immediately began the collection of UFO reports. [4]

We believe this move by Truman was done to help control the UFO phenomenon through the change to the Eisenhower administration.

After the 1952 wave of UFO sightings, the number reduced in 1953, but still happened fairly often. According to the "UFO Hypothesis and Survival Questions," report, "In one three-month period in 1953, (June, July and August) Air Force records show thirty-five sightings whose nature could not be determined." [1]

We believe this indicates that the government somehow made contact with the entities that buzzed Washington D.C.

We believe Eisenhower met with aliens at least three times. It has been reported that one meeting in February of 1954 was held at Edwards Air Force Base in California, and two more meetings were held later at Holloman Air Force Base in New Mexico. [43]

In the first meeting, Eisenhower met with two blue-eyed, Nordic-appearing aliens. They agreed to a treaty to continue the government policy of secrecy in regard to UFO activity and to not interfere with their surveillance and abduction program, all in exchange for some limited access to advanced technology. However, the aliens were not able to dissuade the US from nuclear weapons testing.

In 1951, Project Blue Book director Captain Edward J. Ruppelt, met with experts at a Columbus, Ohio, think tank, the Battelle Memorial Institute, to sponsor a study to be done on UFOs called "Project Blue Book Special Report No. 14."

The study, which was completed in 1954, was the largest investigation ever compiled by the US Air Force.

Four scientific analysts were employed who broke down UFO sightings into knowns, unknowns and cases with insufficient information. Only two of the analysts were needed to agree to the "known" category, but all four were required for the case to be deemed "unknown," so the criteria for an unknown classification had to be unanimous.

After analyzing 3,200 cases the report found that 69 percent of the cases could be classified as "known" or explainable events and 21.5 percent were found to be "unknown."

When the Air Force made the report public in October of 1955, it claimed that the report proved that UFOs did not exist and the secretary of the Air Force claimed only 3 percent of the cases were found to be "unknown." [19]

Federal marshal and chaplain Dr. Frank E. Stranges wrote a book called *Stranger at the Pentagon* in which he describes a three-year visit to the US by an alien named Valiant Thor who claimed to have come from Venus. He appeared to be a Caucasian, red-haired human, and was supposed to have landed in a scout ship on March 16, 1957, in a field in Alexandria, Virginia, requesting an audience with President Eisenhower. In the book, Thor claimed to have been sent by the "high council" because our nuclear capabilities had become a concern to the "galactic community."

Project Blue Book was supposed to have ended on December 17, 1969, but we now know that this government program has never really ended, it just morphed into differently named programs, a recent one of which is called the Advanced Aerospace Threat Identification Program (AATIP). UFO cover ups and disinformation campaigns continued unabated, carried out by the men in black, government agents with no obvious departmental affiliation that showed up to UFO incidents to continue the operations of Project Blue Book. These agents responded to UFO sightings to first question witnesses about what they'd seen, then browbeat them into silence, continuing Project Blue Book's policy of first gathering information, then debunking the events. [21] [44]

This men-in-black response to UFO activity was reported hundreds of times. A mass sighting event would occur in a small town somewhere and these agents dressed in black suits, bearing no insignia, showing no identification or credentials would descend on the town, grill witnesses for information then begin the ridicule, intimidate and discrediting procedure to hush up the event. In sighting events too large for this policy to be effective, a fake investigation would "find" some ludicrous explanation like "it was a weather balloon" or "it was swamp gas."

MASS SIGHTINGS

UFO sightings number in the hundreds of thousands and reporting on them all would fill a thousand books. Here we have included some of the mass sightings that have taken place in the US over the years:

There was a mass UFO sighting over an area of Massachusetts called the Bridgewater Triangle on May 10, 1760. A huge number of European colonists in the towns of Roxbury and Bridgewater saw a sphere of fire streak across the sky. [45]

The New York Herald-Tribune reported on a mass sighting over Chicago on April 9, 1897. A giant, cigar-shaped airship was seen by thousands of witnesses from 8 p.m. to 2 a.m. [4]

New York to Chicago, Dec. 22, 1909. Major newspapers from New York to Chicago had the reported sighting on their front pages. They said thousands of witnesses saw a huge airship flying across the nation. Witnesses thought the ship crashed west of Chicago, but the wreckage was not found. [23]

A mass USO sighting took place off an Aleutian island in the summer of 1945. Crew members of the US transport ship Delarof saw a large round object emerge from the water off the island of Adak. The craft rose straight up out of the water, hovered, then circled the boat three times before zooming off in a southerly direction. The incident lasted about seven to eight minutes. The crew were sworn to secrecy, but in 1968 the boat's radioman Robert S. Crawford reported the incident to the National Investigations Committee On Aerial Phenomena (NICAP). [4]

Hundreds of people saw a large disc-shaped object on Nov. 16, 1952, in Landrum, South Carolina. The incident was also witnessed by an air-traffic controller. [4]

Many people in Rapid City, South Dakota, and in Bismarck, North Dakota, witnessed a fast moving, bright, bluish UFO on August 12 and 13, 1953. It was tracked by radar at Ellsworth Air Force Base. It was followed by F-84 jets as it headed towards Bismarck where it was seen by many more witnesses. [4]

What witnesses describe as a meteor or a ball of fire was seen by thousands of people flying across the US on April 18, 1962, which either landed or crashed at Nellis Air Force Base near Las Vegas, Nevada. It was seen flying over New York, Kansas, Colorado and Eureka, Utah; where it reportedly landed and took off again. At the same time the whole town experienced a power outage. At Reno, Nevada, the object took a sharp left turn and flew south to Las Vegas. Obviously meteors do not make turns, nor do they land and take off again. Witnesses included airline pilots who saw the object below them. [4]

On February 21, 1973, in Piedmont, Missouri, five hundred people claimed to see multi-colored UFO lights hovering over the town. Men in black arrived at the town and started a discrediting campaign, but the sighting was so widespread that the government had to come up with another tactic. A scientist who had been involved in Project Blue Book explained the sighting away as "plasma gas" and "mass hysteria." [21]

A large "V" shaped UFO was seen during a New Year's Eve celebration on December 31, 1982, in Kent, New York. It was seen by a large crowd of revelers enjoying the outdoor festivities. The craft had red, green and white lights which turned all white and increased in brightness. The Hudson Valley is another UFO hotspot with many sightings and abduction reports. [47]

What is now referred to as the Anchorage Incident, took place on November 17, 1986. A Japan JAL airliner, flying from Paris to Tokyo, was harassed by three UFOs, one of which was four times the size of the airliner. The pilots became so alarmed they requested permission for an emergency landing at Anchorage, Alaska. Air traffic controllers at the airport confirmed the sighting on radar. The CIA confiscated all the data and swore the controllers to secrecy. [48]

One of the most famous mass sightings is the Phoenix Lights. On March 13, 1997, between 7:30 and 10:30 p.m. thousands of people witnessed a huge "V-shaped," or "triangular-shaped" UFO slowly flying over 300 miles of Nevada and Arizona, starting from southern Nevada, through the Phoenix area to near Tucson in Arizona where it headed into the Mexican state of Sonora. The lie explaining this one was "flares dropped;" another whopper. Flares slowly descend to the ground, they don't fly horizontally in formation for over 300 miles. The UFO was seen by the Governor of Arizona, Fife Symington. He was a pilot and retired Air Force officer. To make light of the event, he brought out an aide dressed as an alien at a press conference. He didn't acknowledge his encounter at first because he did not want to start a panic, but ten years later he spoke in a press conference about what he witnessed, saying he believed the lights were extraterrestrial. He was very close to the object, and he said he was able to see through it to the stars above. [49]

On July 14, 2001, on the New Jersey Turnpike, lights in a "V" formation were seen near midnight by New Jersey and New York residents. [23]

On January 8, 2008, in Stephenville, Texas, a small dairy-farming town about 100 miles southwest of Dallas, had reported sightings from dozens of witnesses who saw white lights forming first an arc, then vertical parallel lines traveling about 3,000 miles per hour. The witnesses heard no sound. The military explained this one as F-16s flying nearby at the Brownwood Military Operating Area, but everyone knows that these planes are far from silent, and do not fly at those speeds. The witnesses did not believe this explanation. [45]

TWO IMPORTANT SIGHTINGS

One compelling incident includes the sighting of a traffic cop named Lonnie Zamora in Socorro, New Mexico. The incident happened at 5:45 p.m. on April 24, 1964. Zamora claimed to have investigated a loud roaring sound he heard, thinking it might have been an explosion from a dynamite shack. When he arrived on the scene he saw a white, shiny, smooth, oval-shaped UFO sitting on legs on the ground, and saw what he at first thought were two children in white coveralls. The "children" appeared to be "examining or repairing the craft." Zamora said that the craft had a red insignia on it. [50]

When the "children" spotted him they hurried back into the craft. A flame appeared under the object and it took off and flew away. During the take off, Zamora ran away and threw himself to the ground and later called for backup.

FBI and military personnel from White Sands Proving Ground scrambled to the scene within two hours and Project Blue Book scientist

Allen Hynek arrived the next day. Hynek and other government personnel interviewed the rattled police officer and then Zamora was instructed to keep quiet about certain aspects of his account; especially about seeing the "children" and the insignia he saw on the craft. Rock samples at the site appeared to have been melted by a heat source and this was later confirmed in a government lab.

Project Blue Book claimed the incident was unexplained, but most likely was a prototype NASA lunar lander.

Another compelling sighting makes our list because of the photographic evidence and the thorough investigation by LIUFON.

On September 28, 1989, a family of witnesses claimed to have seen a joint military and police force helicopter response to a downed UFO on Smith's Point Beach at Moriches Bay, Long Island, New York, and a giant mothership with six huge lights in the sky hovering above; estimated between 574 feet long or larger. Four military and two Suffolk County Police helicopters spent two-and-a-half hours circling the two ships. The incident was investigated by LIUFON who acquired witness testimony and 48 photographs. [23] [46]

TWO OF THE MOST FAMOUS ABDUCTION STORIES

On September 19, 1961, the now famous abduction incident of Betty and Barney Hill took place. While driving on Route 3 at about 11 p.m. near Lancaster, New Hampshire, on their way home to Portsmouth, they saw what they thought was a bright star in the southwest sky. The light began to snake around and Betty thought it had a pancake shape. [22] [51]

At this point the couple experienced missing time and memory blocks.

Betty suffered from nightmares after the event.

A few years later, the couple consulted a psychiatrist and under separate hypnotic regressions so as not to hear each other's accounts, they both related the same story.

The light took up a position above the road ahead of their car. The object was a flying saucer. Barney stopped the car and got out to view the object through binoculars. He saw alien figures in the windows of the ship. Then he jumped back in the car and sped off, but before they got very far, their car began to vibrate.

The ship landed in front of their car. They describe aliens, later known as the Greys, who took them from their car.

They were taken on board an alien ship. Betty pleaded with her captors to not hurt her. Then she suffered great pain when they inserted a needle into her stomach.

Barney had skin and sperm samples taken from him.

Transcripts of their regressions were written up by journalist John Fuller called "An Interrupted Journey."

The Hill incident is just one of tens of thousands of these kinds of reports. We know that people are being abducted by UFOs, having genetic material taken from them and then the abductees are returned. We know that these people are usually taken many times; sometimes hundreds of times over their lifespans. These abductees always have their memories tampered with in order to either forget their abductions, or to have different memories implanted in their minds; distorting their memories of these events.

We know that the Greys are abducting women, impregnating them and then in a few months are re-abducting them to take the unborn fetuses. This has happened thousands of times. The women are frequently taken again and introduced to their alien/human hybrid offspring.

We believe they are using this breeding program to create beings able to move among us undetected, and that these undercover agents look identical to humans, but have the ability to read minds and to some extent control the minds of ordinary humans.

We are learning about this practice from therapists doing regression work with abductees, especially from Professor David M. Jacobs, who has done thousands of regressions and written several books on the subject. [52]

THE TRAVIS WALTON ABDUCTION

The Travis Walton abduction is another famous event, told in detail in his book, *The Walton Experience*, and in a movie called *Fire in the Sky* in which a writer wrote a "flashier story" for Walton's experiences on the ship. [53] [54] [55]

Walton, a 22-year-old man from Snowflake, Arizona, was traveling in a pickup truck with six other workers on Nov. 5, 1975. The crew had spent a long day logging in the mountains.

Driving back to town through the Apache-Sitgreaves National Forest in Arizona, they saw a light moving through the trees. When the ship crossed the road in front of them, they saw a large metallic disk above them in the sky.

Walton got out of the truck to get a closer look. His coworkers saw him get hit by a ray of bluish light from the hovering ship that threw him back to the ground. They took off in terror leaving Walton behind. After a few minutes the crew got their terror under control and they returned to retrieve Walton, but he and the ship were gone.

In his testimony of what happened to him on the ship, Walton said he found himself on an elevated operating table in a hospital-like room. He looked into the face of a Grey alien and there were other Greys in the room. He panicked and began fighting. The Greys left the room and were replaced by human-looking aliens, when he saw the more human-like faces, he became more calm. They led him to another room where they put a mask over his face and he blacked out.

When the crew reported the incident to police. Navajo County Sheriff Marlin Gillespie conducted a search, but they found no trace of Walton.

The crew were given lie detector tests which all but one of them passed the first time, and all of them passed the second time. Walton himself also passed a lie detector test.

The police didn't know what to believe, some thought the crew may have murdered Walton and made up this crazy story.

Walton was returned five days later outside the nearby town of Herber. He found himself lying on the ground in the dark with a light above him. He saw the bottom of the craft right before it shot up into the sky. The authorities dismissed the incident as a hallucination.

We believe Walton first saw Grey aliens and later saw the Nordics. We believe the aliens had planned to keep Walton and he would have ended up as a missing, never to be found person. We believe it's likely the aliens monitor our news programs and decided to return Walton because of the huge media sensation caused by the witnesses.

We know the Project Blue Book secrecy policy continued for about seven decades, only recently has the government been releasing some military videos to the public, proving once and for all that they have been lying to us about UFO activity all these years.

Most alien encounters are reported to be with the race of the Greys, the Reptilians or the Nordics, who appear to be humans, but are very pale and tall and are sometimes described as having slightly glowing skin.

The Greys come in a few varieties, the very short pale gray-colored ones, the slighting taller and slimmer grayish-yellow colored variety and sometimes very tall spindly ones. All these varieties are humanoid with two arms, legs, eyes, nostrils, feet and hands with between four and six fingers. Some rare photographic evidence of Grey aliens in human captivity show them having two nipples as well, suggesting they evolved from lactating mammals. [55]

In a video deathbed confession made by Boyd Bushman, a senior scientist with Lockheed Martin, on June 17, 2014, he claims to have received extraterrestrial material from senior staff at Area 51 for the purpose of reverse engineering their technology. Bushman claimed the US government has eighteen Grey alien individuals in captivity. During his confession, he held up a photograph of a Grey alien. In addition to the extra large head, tiny ears and black eyes, the alien appears to have a very thin chest, a sternum, pectorals and nipples. [24]

We know that people have been disappearing in the thousands every year. Some disappearances are eventually explained, but thousands have never been solved. According to the National Missing and Unidentified Persons database there are over 17,000 missing person cases currently open in the US. We surmise that some of the cases that were never solved are because they were abductees that for whatever reason were never returned. [56]

THE ANIMAL MUTILATIONS

We know that UFO activity is frequently associated with the thousands of reported animal mutilation events. Wikipedia describes these mutilations as, "the killing and mutilation of cattle under unusual, usually bloodless circumstances. This phenomenon has been observed among wild animals as well. Worldwide, sheep, horses, goats, pigs, rabbits, cats, dogs, bison, deer and elk have been reported mutilated with similar bloodless excisions; often an ear, eyeball, jaw flesh, tongue, lymph nodes, genitals and rectum are removed." [45][57]

The blood of the animals is also missing.

The organs are carved out with perfect surgical precision and cauterized at the same time. No footprints of people or predators are ever found around the carcasses. The sky-facing eyes are removed in a perfect circular cut.

There is one very strange report of an animal mutilation site in Alaska involving many wild animals, including an elk, which is not indigenous to the area, and a killer whale corpse though the site was far inland.

Animal mutilation incidents in the US number in the hundreds of thousands and worldwide in the millions.

After thousands of mutilations occurred in the 1970s, pressure mounted on officials to do something and in 1979 the FBI opened an investigation. In January of 1980 the FBI closed its case blaming the events on predators.

This conclusion is clearly ludicrous. Predatory animals leave tracks, they leave jagged, tearing wounds, they do not remove organs with bloodless, surgical precision, they do not cauterize wounds and they do not extract and remove blood. We believe this stupid report is further evidence of Project Blue Book's lying and discrediting policy.

PROMISED PROOF IS PULLED

During a visit to Norton Air Force Base, filmmaker Robert Emenegger was approached by Paul Shartle, the base's audio-visual director, to make a documentary on UFOs. Emenegger was promised real footage of a meeting between aliens and Holloman Air Force Base personnel. Emenegger made the documentary, but at the last minute permission to get the promised footage was rescinded. Emenegger went ahead with the documentary and released it without the block-buster ending he'd been promised. The film, and the book of the same name, was called *UFOs, Past, Present & Future.* Even without the film, the documentary caused a big stir.

In an Eyes on Cinema interview that can be seen on YouTube, Shartle, who had actually seen the film, gives a description. [58] [59]

In a Facebook post the Eyes on Cinema interview transcript is posted and further details were added.

Shartle said, "I saw footage of three disc-shaped crafts. One of the crafts landed and two of them went away. It appeared to be in trouble because it oscillated all the way down to the ground. However, it did land on three pods. A sliding door opened, a ramp extended, and out came three aliens. They were human size. They had odd gray complexions and a pronounced nose. They wore tight-fitting jumpsuits, headdresses that appeared to be communication devices and in their hands they held a translator, I was told."

The post said the Holloman base commander Ellis Lloyd Richards Jr. and other Air Force officers went out to meet them.

Shartle said they were big-nosed tall humanoids with gray complexions and eyes with vertical slits similar to cat eyes. They had thin slit-like mouths and no chins.

The documentary did have eight seconds of actual footage from the meeting, but it only shows a bright light approaching the base from far away.

Emenegger said he gave a copy to Steven Spielberg and it became the influence for his film *Close Encounters of the Third Kind*. Emenegger's film screened in 1975, and Spielberg's came out in 1977.

ASTRONAUT AND COSMONAUT WITNESSES

We know that NASA astronauts and Russian cosmonauts have seen and reported UFO activity.

In May of 1963, during the final Mercury mission, Astronaut Gordon Cooper, piloting the spacecraft Faith 7, reported seeing a bright green, glowing object fly by his spacecraft on his final orbit. [60]

On December 4, 1965, during the Gemini 7 mission, Jim Lovell and Frank Borman reported a boogie, which was definitely NOT the booster rocket, since they were able to see the booster as well. The craft was described as cigar-like. [60]

We know that in June of 1969 the Apollo 11 spacecraft was tracked by a UFO on its way to the moon. Buzz Aldrin has described this in many interviews. [60]

In a book *Our Cosmic Ancestors,* written by NASA communication specialist Maurice Chatelain, he reported that Neil Armstrong and Buzz Aldrin were being watched by two UFOs while they were walking on the moon. There is a two-minute gap in the moon landing footage that NASA claims was due to a camera-overheating problem. He also claimed that all the Apollo and Gemini missions were followed by UFOs.

On the Salyut 7 Space Station, July 12, 1984, Soviet cosmonauts Oleg Atkov, Leonid Kizim and Vladimir Solovyov claimed they saw seven enormous, glowing, winged angel-like beings outside their space station. These beings were described as the size of a jet plane. The cosmonauts said that instead of feeling afraid, the creatures gave them a strange sense of well being. They hovered for several minutes before disappearing. [61]

March 13, 1989, on the Space Shuttle Discovery, an astronaut sent a message to NASA on an open channel. Shuttle Commander Colonel John Blaha, said "we still have the alien spacecraft under observance." This time it's not a boogie or a UFO or a UAP, it's an "alien spacecraft."[60]

Red lights were seen by astronauts on Skylab. The space station was launched on May 25, 1973. After it had been in orbit for about four months, astronaut Owen Garriott saw oscillating red lights out the window. The photo he took looked a bit like the description of the "space angels" seen in 1984 from the Salyut 7. [62]

During the NASA space shuttle Columbia STS-80 mission between the launch of November 19, 1996, and the landing on December 7 of the same year, veteran astronaut Story Musgrave shot a video of round, white lights in orbit, performing like UFOs; making instantaneous, at-speed-directional changes. Earlier on the recording, there is a flyby of something that looks like a swimming sperm moving at 680 miles per second. [62]

ALIENS ARE INTERESTED IN NUKES

Aliens have a particular interest in nuclear facilities. This interest has been well documented by researcher and author Robert Hastings in his book *UFOs & Nukes: Extraordinary Encounters at Nuclear Weapons Sites.* Hastings interviewed over 150 veterans in relation to UFO sightings and activities near nuclear facilities. [63] [64]

He co-organized a CNN press conference, with former Air Force Commander and Air Force Nuclear Launch Officer Robert Salas, at the National Press Club to inform the public on September 27, 2010, in Washington D.C.

At this conference, seven former Air Force officers discussed UFO incidents that occurred at their nuclear bases, including Salas, Ret. Air Force Colonel Charles Halt, Ret. Navy Commander Master Chief Patrick McDonough, former Air Force Captain Robert Jamison and Ret. Air Force Lt. Colonel Dwynne Arneson.

Salas had been ringside at the most disturbing event described at the conference; the Malmstrom Incident. On March 16, 1967, at the nuclear missile facility Malmstrom Air Force Base in Montana, UFOs took all ten nuclear missiles off line. In the early morning hours before dawn, witnesses reported seeing very bright lights moving in the sky. One of the lights took up a position just outside the security fence. Then one at a time the missiles went off line until all ten had been deactivated. All of the witnesses were forced to sign non-disclosure agreements.

OTHER INCIDENTS INVOLVING NUKES INCLUDE:

In September of 1964, during the first inter-continental ballistic missile test at Vandenberg Air Force Base, California, a UFO was seen following the missile at 11,000 miles per hour, shooting some kind of beam at the dummy warhead and causing the missile to burn up in the atmosphere. The CIA came and confiscated the film footage. [22] [63] [64]

In 1968 at Minot Air Force Base in North Dakota, a UFO moved a twenty-ton steel and concrete cover over one of the missile silos. [63]

After the first Trinity nuclear bomb test on July 16, 1945, in Alamogordo, New Mexico, green fireballs began buzzing the area. These green orbs were sighted time after time at nuclear tests.

On June 24, 1947, pilot Kenneth Arnold saw nine flying saucers near Mount Rainier in Washington, only a few miles away from the Hanford Nuclear Facility, the US's first plutonium processing plant. The now famous incident marked the first time the term "flying saucer" was coined. Arnold was flying his new-model Callair plane north from Chehalis, Washington, when he saw a line of nine, shiny disks flying in formation. He thought the objects were at least one hundred feet across, and was surprised they had no tails or wings. He calculated the objects were traveling at about 1,000 miles per hour. Project Blue Book recorded the case as a "mirage." [63]

In the late 1940s all four of the US nuclear weapons development labs reported UFO sightings.

The Roswell incident took place a stone's throw away from Roswell Air Force Base, home to the 509th Bomb Wing that dropped the bombs on Hiroshima and Nagasaki. [63]

We know that UFOs are radioactive and that people who come in contact with UFOs frequently exhibit signs of radiation sickness. We believe the aliens are using nuclear power in their aircraft. [65]

The US branch of the British tabloid The Sun made a FOIA request in December of 2017 that was finally complied with on April 5, 2022. The Defense Intelligence Agency released a 1,574-page Pentagon report, part of which detailed injuries such as electromagnetic radiation burns, brain and nervous system damage and unaccounted for pregnancies after UFO encounters.[65]

UFO AND USO FACTS

In 1952 Coral and Jim Lorenzen founded the Aerial Phenomenon Research Organization or APRO and began to collect thousands of UFO reports from all over the world, cross referencing and collating types of incidents. Their organization grew to have thousands of members. Scientists and military people joined the group. MUFON is a spin-off organization from APRO. MUFON now has thousands of members. [66]

We know that the majority of abductees have green or hazel eyes (a mutation in humans) and have Rh negative blood (also thought to be a mutation). Between three and four out of 10 reported abductees are Rh negative. [51]

We know that UFOs come in a wide variety of sizes and shapes, but all of them exhibit at least one of the following characteristics: supersonic speed (in both air and water), the ability to stop and hover, apparently in defiance of gravity, the ability to instantly change their direction without needing to slow down, the ability to enter and exit bodies of water, easily shifting from airborne to submersible at will, the ability to cloak themselves and disappear from view to the naked eye while sometimes still registering on radar or infrared, the ability to interfere with and shutdown our electronics, the ability to instantly reach their high speeds without gradually increasing to that speed, exhibit no known means of propulsion and whatever propulsion being used is silent or sometimes described as a low humming sound that is felt more than heard.

An NSA report stated, "Sometimes the phenomena appear to defy radar and to cause massive electromagnetic interferences." [1 67]

We know that aliens are interested in particular human blood lines and the abduction phenomenon tends to run in families. [52]

We know that UFOs are frequently seen over ancient megalithic structures.

We know that UFOs can also be USOs that can move at high speeds underwater.

One example of this is an incident that took place in February of 1963. While conducting anti-submarine maneuvers off the Puerto Rico trench off the north coast of the island, the USS Wasp aircraft carrier tracked a USO over the course of four days. The unknown sonar target was clocked at a speed of 150 knots and had descended to a depth of 27,000 feet. At the time, the top speed of a US submarine was forty-five knots and they were only able to reach a depth of three thousand feet. Members of the carrier group tried chasing the object, but were unable to catch it. Even now, there is no submarine capable of this speed. Thirteen captains entered the incident in their ship's logs.

We know that alien bases have been discovered on Antarctica and a huge no-fly zone has been created to hide them.

We know that UFO activity is frequently regional, with clusters of different sightings taking place in the same area.

We believe that aliens have been playing God in their human interactions for many centuries, and have only stopped doing this as we became sophisticated enough for the tactic to stop working.

We know that aliens are telepathic and there have been thousands of reports of them communicating with abductees non-verbally.

In the modern age, everyone now has a video-camera phone in their pocket, and can instantly upload and distribute these videos to the world. Television shows are popping up showing this video evidence and interviewing witnesses. There have also been more mass sighting events, with hundreds of videos, that now make government cover-ups impossible.

On December 30, 2013, former Canadian Minister of National Defense Paul Hellyer appeared on the RT TV network and informed the public that aliens have been visiting earth for thousands of years. He said they belong to a federation and that they have rules about interfering with us. [69]

CHAPTER TWO

RECENT DISCLOSURES AND A NEW GOVERNMENT POLICY

In 2017 retired special AATIP agent Luis Elizondo released three classified videos of military UFO encounters to the *New York Times*, and then later started his own UFO investigating television show called *Unidentified: Inside America's UFO Investigation*. The now famous videos are called, "Tic Tac," "go fast" and "gimbal." [67]

The Times article by Helene Cooper, Ralph Blumenthal and Leslie Kean was titled "Glowing Auras and 'Black Money': The Pentagon's Mysterious U.F.O. Program."

Prior to this article the Pentagon had never released any of this type of information from this agency, which was formed to analyze and report UAP incidents to the Defense Department.

Elizondo had been an intelligence officer for decades before taking over the AATIP program in 2009.

In his TV show, Elizondo described UAPs as having one or all of what he calls the "observables" abilities not shared by any known aircraft. He said they display anti-gravity (flying with no apparent means of propulsion), instantaneous acceleration at G-forces that would kill a human being, hypersonic velocity (sometimes over five times the speed of sound), low observability (the ability to cloak or disappear), trans-medium travel (the ability to move between space, air and water while flying). [67]

The Tic Tac incident took place in November of 2004 off the California coast about 100 miles southwest of San Diego, and was documented by pilots from the aircraft carrier USS Nimitz and three attending vessels of the carrier group, the Vincennes, Chosin and Princeton. The group was holding exercises with VFA-41 fighter jets and holding mock fighting drills.

This incident is the most documented and corroborated UAP event in history.

Six Navy fighter jet pilots spotted and chased a white, oval-shaped UFO and took the now famous video. During this encounter, an underwater USO was also tracked.

The Princeton tracked an object at 80,000 feet which fell at lightning speed to right above the ocean; hovering over roiling water as if something was in the water underneath the "Tic Tac."

Two fighter jets had launched from the USS Nimitz to perform maneuvers, one of the jets was being flown by squadron commander David M. Fravor and the other by Lt. Commander Alex Dietrich.

The chief radar specialist, Senior Chief Petty Officer Kevin Day, on the USS Princeton interrupted the maneuver and dispatched the jets to the UFO's coordinates for a real-world intercept.

When the jets arrived at the coordinates, they saw water churning and at first the pilots thought something had crashed in the ocean. Then an approximately forty-foot-long, white, "giant Tic-Tac-shaped object," with no markings, wings, windows, intakes or exhaust, appeared above the object in the water. The UAP began moving in instantaneous, erratic motions as if it perceived the presence of the jets. The jet pilots attempted to intercept it, but it crossed their bow and accelerated away at about 3,700 mile per hour, reappearing on radar sixty miles away.

Another jet was launched with a targeting pod and infrared camera and this jet took the actual "Tic Tac" video.

Day said he tracked many of these objects dropping down from the upper atmosphere, which then moved south in a formation at 28,000 feet traveling at 100 knots, which is usually considered too slow to be able to fly at that altitude.

One of the objects was tracked diving into the water and accelerating away at seventy knots, which is much faster than any manmade submersible craft.

The UAP activity was tracked by the Navy's most advanced radar system, the Aegis Spy-1. The technicians thought the system might have been malfunctioning, so they rebooted the computer and found the UAPs were still there, and then confirmation reports came in from other ships.

Naval officers collected and "disappeared" the hard drives with the recordings on them until they were later released to the public by Elizondo.

The "go fast" and "gimbal" videos were both shot by naval jets from the nuclear aircraft carrier USS Theodore Roosevelt in 2015 off the coast of Jacksonville, Florida. Both videos were shot in infrared with the UFOs showing no heat signatures.

Prior to the videos being taken, jet pilots with a squadron called the Red Rippers flying out of Naval Air Station Oceana in Virginia were experiencing encounters with many UAPs during their exercises beginning in the summer of 2014. During their maneuvers up and down the eastern seaboard the pilots were seeing strange radar tracks and initially thought there might be something wrong with their upgraded radar system until they actually witnessed the UAPs themselves. The pilots described seeing a cube inside a sphere and also various round objects flashing around them. Over a period of months, into 2015, pilots reported seeing strange objects nearly every time they flew.

When one of the objects flew between two jets at very close range, nearly causing a mid-air collision, the pilots submitted a safety report to the Navy Safety Center.

The "go fast" video is of a round, white craft moving at blazing speed, roughly two-thirds the speed of sound, just above the surface of the ocean. In the accompanying audio you can hear the pilots are amazed at how fast the object is moving and confused as to what it could be. The craft has no wings, no visible means of propulsion or lift and displays no heat signature.

The "gimbal" video is just part of a longer recording of a squadron of five small round UAPs flying in formation with the larger gimbal object traveling behind them. That's why the chatter in the video describes seeing a "fleet of them" even though only one object is seen in the released video. It was described as a hovering gyroscope holding position against 120 knots of wind that then rotates over ninety degrees on its axis with no change to its altitude.

These UAP objects are all displaying abilities that defy the laws of physics. They are moving at instantaneous velocities at hypersonic speeds without creating sonic booms, making high-G turns no human pilot would be able to survive then flying at speeds so slow an aircraft would not be able to stay in the air. They can stop on a dime and hover. They can move effortlessly through trans-mediums, plunging into water and emerging from water before speeding off at thousands of miles per hour.

The lack of sonic booms in dumbfounding. It's almost as if they are carving out a portal and moving through that, instead of through the atmosphere, causing no air pressure as they move.

No explanation ever emerged after these videos were taken and the safety reports submitted until Elizondo leaked them to the media.

All three of the Elizondo videos can easily be viewed in several locations online.

We are mostly sticking to US incidents, but this is a very well documented case that took place in Mexico. On March 5, 2004, off the Yucatan Peninsula of Mexico, the Mexican Air Force spotted and recorded an incident with eleven white lights that appeared on infrared and radar. They were traveling at very high speed, tracking along with the jets. The jets were moving at 200 miles per hour, but the lights were sticking with them and flying around them. After the incident the Mexican government held a press conference admitting that UFOs exist. [60]

We believe these released videos and the changes to how people record and disseminate information have forced the government to adopt a new strategy in relation to UFOs. We believe the new position is to release limited UFO information to the public, while pretending to be as baffled about it as we are. The "gosh, gee, we admit these things exist, but we have no idea what they are" strategy. Since the government is known to be hiding actual crashed UFOs, actual dead alien bodies (and maybe some live ones), we believe this strategy is another disingenuous, bald-faced lie, but one that lets the government pretend to be a cooperating participant in the search for the truth.

Evidence of this new strategy comes in the form of the Pentagon declassifying and officially releasing the three previously-released Elizondo videos with a statement by the Department of Defense confirming the authenticity of the videos, but they stopped short of claiming them to be from extraterrestrial sources. [71]

Along with the release they issued this statement, "The Department of Defense is releasing the videos in order to clear up any misconception by the public on whether or not the footage that has been circulating was real, or whether or not there is more to the videos. The aerial phenomena observed in the videos remain characterized as 'unidentified.'"

Another pair of leaked videos of a 2019 incident off the California coast, that the government later confirmed as real, showed pyramidal-shaped UFOs flying over the USS Russell and an infrared video taken by the USS Omaha showing a "Tic Tac" trans-medium UFO splashing into the water. The videos were posted by documentary filmmaker Jeremy Corbell.

On June 25, 2021, the Office of the Director of National Intelligence released a report, "Preliminary Assessment: Unidentified Aerial Phenomena." Though the report never claims the UFOs are under extraterrestrial control, it does confirm that UFO, or UAP, activity is not coming from Russia or China or any other Earth government. The report examined 144 incidents and only found one to be a large, deflating balloon. All the other cases remained "unexplained." Most of the events involved first-hand witness reports by military aviators, and systems they deemed reliable.

The report says the phenomenon requires further study and we may have to increase our scientific knowledge to be able to understand what is going on.

We believe the release of this report is further evidence of our assessment of the new government position concerning UFOs, or what we referred to before as the "gosh, gee, we admit these things exist, but we have no idea what they are" policy.

All of the incidents in these two chapters would each fill a book, in fact there are hundreds of books about them. Except for briefly touching on these subjects where needed, this book will not go into the details of this knowledge, but will rather take much of it as "given," for the sake of arguing our theories.

Understand that for every incident that took place here in the US there is a similar incident or set of incidents in almost every country on the globe. But, we believe that after World War II, because of the use of nuclear weapons, the US and later Russia, were the particular focus of UFO activity.

CHAPTER THREE

WHERE ARE THEY HIDING?

Where are they? Most people who believe UFOs to be controlled by aliens, believe that they are visiting here from another planet. There are roughly 10,000 world-wide reported UFO sightings per year; every year. That is REPORTED sightings. Given how people who report UFOs are laughed at and ridiculed, the number who don't report them is probably very high.

With so many occurrences, doesn't it seem unlikely that they are just visiting?

If we assume they are visiting aliens, we must then also assume that it is incredibly easy for them to come here. So easy that they visit 10,000 times a year. In our opinion this stresses credulity. It is our supposition that the people flying around in UFOs are NOT visiting. They live here. They are in residence.

If as we surmise, the beings are in residence, then we have to ask ourselves, where are they? Where are they hiding? The answer to this question is, they are hiding underground. We believe there is sufficient evidence to prove they reside in underground, carved-out, tempera-ture-controlled bases inside our planet.

In current ufology circles, reports have been buzzing about under-ground bases, underground cities and hollowed-out mountains. Some-times they are reportedly run by contingents of alien and human military personnel, sometimes the Grey and Reptilian races of aliens are involved and sometimes the aliens are described as superhuman, or advanced humans. In some of these bases there are reports of experimentations and even dissections being done on human subjects. [72]

This is obviously very disturbing. The idea that some of our missing persons have ended up in pieces on cold slabs after having been confronted by alien faces while they were totally paralyzed and completely defenseless is a horrifying thought; a scene that only belongs in a horror film. The supposition that this is being done with the participation, or at least acquiescence, of our own government only adds to the horror; it is the ultimate betrayal. If this is really taking place, one need look no further for a motivation for our government to cover up their joint military/alien activities.

It is our opinion that President Truman and President Eisenhower after him, justified this deal by telling themselves that the alien technology would be worth it. The sacrifice of a few individuals would be justified because the tech would give our military an edge and would save more lives in battle than would be otherwise lost to war; but if this evil pact was ever really entered into, it would be something that could never, ever be disclosed to the public. This knowledge would have to be protected; even murdered for. After all, what are a few more lives when you've already sanctioned the ultimate betrayal?

Archuleta Mesa near Dulce, New Mexico, is said to be one of these underground, joint alien/military bases. It is known to the UFO community and the local Jicarilla Apache people who reside there, as Dulce Air Force Base. Mount Hayes in Alaska is also believed to be a joint alien/military base and there are rumblings about another joint base that has a huge underground dark pyramid within 100 miles of Mount Hayes. Other suspected bases include Mount Shasta in California, Mount Adams in Washington, Brown Mountain in North Carolina, Mount Kailash in Tibet and Mount Bugarach in France as they are all hotbeds of UFO sightings. We believe there are joint alien/military bases in Antarctica as well. [72][73][74][75]

We also think there is an alien base in the hills near Skinwalker Ranch in Utah, which is currently being investigated by a team of scientists who are making their findings public on a television show called, *The Secret of Skinwalker Ranch.*

Some people believe there are alien bases hidden in Earth's bodies of water. UFOs have been seen emerging from lakes in Peru and from out of our oceans.

The supporting evidence to these claims is thin because these are some of the government's most carefully guarded secrets, but no matter how thin it is, some evidence does exist.

Anonymous witnesses have testified to a military no-fly zone at the South Pole where there is a huge hole in the ice with a long ice ramp leading into it, and also an octagonal extraterrestrial base, that when entered was temperature controlled, with green walls with hieroglyphs on them, that were lit from an undetermined light source. There is also a satellite photo showing an enormous, flying-saucer-shaped hole in a mountain side that appears to be artificially constructed. [73]

UNDERGROUND ALIEN BASES

The most famous of the supposed joint alien/US military bases is Dulce Air Force Base.

The secret Dulce facility is said to be two miles underground, seven levels deep and the lower levels are shared by government and alien personnel. [75]

Geologist and explosives engineer Phil Schneider claimed to have been contracted by the US government to do excavations of large areas at the base. According to his testimony, he was working underground to expand the existing base when he, his crew and a group of military personnel were involved in battle with Grey and Reptilian aliens. [74]

Schneider was recorded talking about the incident on May 8, 1995, at a presentation in Post Falls, Idaho.

"I was involved in 1979 in a horrendous firefight with alien/human-type whatever you want to call 'em. And I was one of the survivors, sixty-six secret service agents, FBI and the like, Black Berets, died in that firefight."

In a Huffington Post article he said that while drilling at the Dulce base, he came face-to-face with a seven-foot tall, stinky, Grey alien. He shot two of the aliens and was shot at by another who fired a "laser-plasma ball...which blew off some of his fingers." He went on to allege that a Green Beret gave his life for him.

In an Epoch Times article Schneider claimed the existence of "1,477 underground bases around the world, 129 of which were located in the United States."

Schneider claimed to have later learned about experiments being conducted by extraterrestrials at the base.

"Basically what had occurred was that we surprised a whole under-mountain base of existing aliens and later I was to find out that we are not the highest on the food chains."

Eight months after his presentation, Schneider was found dead in his apartment. He had rubber tubing wrapped around his neck. His death was ruled to be a suicide. [74]

Many UFO investigators believe he was murdered in order to silence him.

On a TV show called *UFO Witness* in their *Aliens Underground* episode, UFO investigator and former federal agent Ben Hansen visited the Archuleta Mesa and spoke with members of the local Jicarilla tribe. The area is a hotbed of UFO sightings and abduction claims of Grey aliens performing experiments on abductees. Witnesses of the area reported seeing a door opening on the mesa, a light spilling out and oval- or egg-shaped UFOs entering and exiting from the door. During the show, Hansen pointed a thermal camera at the ridge where witnesses claimed the door was located and he spotted a significant heat signature coming off the top of the mesa; much hotter than the surrounding rock. [75]

The show tells about a leak from a government security guard in the 1970s and a report called the "Dulce Papers." Tribal police kept a copy of the report and they showed it to Hansen during the program. The papers reveal that in the jointly occupied (US/alien) facility, hundreds of creatures are being grown in tanks called "wombs" inside the underground base, one kilometer below the Archuleta Mesa. The description of the creatures matches what ufologists call the Grey aliens and other beings that appear to be alien/human hybrids. The papers also confirm the base is seven levels deep and is jointly occupied by US military personnel and aliens.

The Jicarilla Apache have stories in their folklore about star people living underground. [75]

MOUNT HAYES, ALASKA

Alaska has a lot of UFO sightings. This state has one of the highest numbers of them and also a very high number of human disappearances; 16,000 Alaskans have gone missing in the past thirty years.

Many of the most credible sightings take place in the center of the state near Fairbanks. About ninety miles from Fairbanks, and thirty-nine miles from the Army base of Fort Greely, is a very large, remote, 14,000 foot high mountain called Mount Hayes. There are hundreds of reports of UFOs in the area, sometimes traveling in large groups. [72]

MUFON ufologists believe Mount Hayes is a joint alien/US military base.

This belief probably originated with the story of Patrick H. Price. [72]

During the height of the Cold War the Soviets began looking into the practice of remote viewing, and anything the Soviets could do, we could do better; right?

So, the CIA began recruiting psychics who were able to separate their consciousness from their bodies, send their consciousness to a place and time and see what was there; this is essentially what remote viewing is.

The CIA called this program Operation Stargate. Working in collaboration with the Stanford Research Institute, remote viewers began spying on the Soviets. Pat Price was a former Burbank, California, police officer who was one of the most skilled of the remote viewers. He began working for the SRI and then later for the CIA.

Remote viewers are sometimes pulled to a place of interest; called an attractor. During a Soviet-located remote viewing mission, Price felt attracted to Mount Hayes. There deep inside the mountain he saw an alien base. He described the aliens as super-advanced humanoids. He also saw regular humans working alongside the aliens.

Since then, other remote viewers have seen the same base, with human experimentations and dissections taking place.

Price wanted to tell the public about his find, but while staying in a Las Vegas hotel, one day after meeting with officials from the National Security Agency, he claimed to be suffering from severe stomach cramps and died. His death was ruled a heart attack. We believe this was another murder to silence a talkative witness.

Price's story is backed up by the strange evidence circulating about the black pyramid in Denali National Park, fifty miles southwest of Mount McKinley (now Mount Denali), uncovered by UFO investigator and journalist Linda Moulton Howe. A former counterintelligence officer, Sgt. Douglas Mutschler, claimed to have discovered a large blank area on a military map when he was deployed to Alaska in 1989. The entire region had been surveyed in detail, but this one spot had been left out. This made him feel as if they were hiding something. [76][77]

Then in 1992, a nuclear bomb test in China sent shockwaves through the crust of the earth and geologists were able to use the wave to get a picture of the Earth's crust. Earthquake monitoring stations in Alaska picked up the waves and were able to analyze them and determine the density of the rock as the waves passed through. They detected an enormous, pyramidal-structure, underground. This pyramid is supposed to be 100 feet taller than the Great Pyramid in Giza. The local Alaska news media ran the story, but it was immediately pulled afterwards and never aired again. Mutschler saw the program and went to the TV station to investigate and found the tapes of the show had been confiscated by "two men." Any further investigations he undertook, were thwarted by military officers. Frustrated by his failed efforts, Mutschler contacted Howe, who reached out to her network of contacts and found another report of the dark pyramid. The son of a military engineer, told her anonymously that his father had seen the pyramid first hand. He told her that mining shaft elevators were set up to access this underground pyramid that was somehow generating a huge amount of energy.

Other rumors of the black pyramid have been reported. It was supposedly discovered by our military; not built by our military. The personnel who are there now, reportedly wear black uniforms with no insignia.

When a radio host investigator named Bruce Pearson flew over the area, he found a partly squared-off clearing, an old road cut through the trees and an old, overgrown air strip.

A woman remote viewer claimed to have "seen" an underground base with a pyramid and reported her sightings to Howe. In her testimony she said the guide in her vision was human-like, but not human. She said the base was deep underground and the pyramid seemed to be an energy source used to charge UFO disks.

These areas of Alaska are very remote, requiring a plane to get close to them. If someone wanted to hide secret bases from the rest of the world, these would be good places to hide them. Both these bases are in the Fairbanks, Alaska, region, within 100 miles of each other. The Fairbanks area is a hotbed of UFO sightings.

Alaska in general is a state with a lot of UFO reports, which is surprising considering the sparse population. UFOs have been seen flying out of volcanoes in the Aleutian Island chain, and USOs have been spotted rising out of the water off the Alaskan coast and they have been seen taking off from animal mutilation sites.

ACTIVITY IN ANTARCTICA

There are reports of alien bases under the ice of the South Pole. Again evidence is thin, frequently provided by anonymous witnesses and rumors, but one hard little kernel of evidence is the weird cosmic rays detected by the Antarctic Impulsive Transient Antenna, (ANITA), launched from McMurdo Station in December of 2006. Cosmic rays are high-energy protons and atomic nuclei and they are commonly detected coming from deep space. But, ANITA detected them coming from below the Antarctic ice; traveling upward. Cosmic rays are not supposed to do this. It then happened again when ANITA was launched in 2014.

When researchers investigated the ANITA data in 2018 they discovered three other similar anomalies in the data from another Antarctica experiment called IceCube. They found the particles were emerging from the ice at angles deemed impossible by Standard Model physics. [78] [79]

ADMIRAL BYRD'S ALIEN CONTACTS

Rear Admiral Richard E. Byrd is at the root of two of the strangest alien encounters of 1947, supposedly taking place at about the same time at opposite ends of the globe.

A Russian documentary, released in 2006, based on a 1947 Soviet intelligence report, described a battle between an American carrier group and flying saucers at the South Pole. The mission was called Operation Highjump and it was commanded by Admiral Byrd. [7]

According to the documentary Admiral Byrd had orders to destroy a Nazi base under the ice in Queen Maud Land, Antarctica.

Before World War II Hitler was showing an inexplicable interest in Antarctica. He dispatched enormous resources to the continent.

The Russian documentary surmised that Hitler's interest in Antarctica may have been spurred by the belief that the continent of Antarctica could be the lost continent of Atlantis. The theory comes from the Admiral Piri Reis map. This map drawn by the admiral in 1513, shows an incredibly accurate rendering of the coastline of Antarctica, but without its polar ice cap. Reis claimed he drew the map from older maps. It was thought that the only possible way the coastline of Antarctica could be accurately drawn without ice had to do with the theory of crustal displacement and the lithospheric shift. There are some who believe the crust of the earth sometimes slips over the liquid mantle of the planet, moving continents quickly. This theory is thought to be the explanation for pole shifting and the evidence that the earth poles sometimes change position.

Other theories claim the continent of Antarctica was once Atlantis and instead of being swallowed by the sea, it just moved to the South Pole and was swallowed by ice instead.

Again according to the documentary, Hitler believed the theory about Atlantis and thought it was the original home of the Aryan race; believing Germany to be the heir to Atlantean technology.

Whatever his reasons may have been, Hitler was undoubtedly interested in Antarctica, so much so that he was willing to commit huge resources to the continent just as he was preparing for war.

In the 1930s Germany mapped out huge areas of Queen Maud Land and U-boats started combing the coast of that region. The U-boats were under the command of Grand Admiral Karl Doenitz. At one point Doenitz claimed, "My submariners have found a true paradise on earth," and later said, "The German submarine fleet is proud, at the other end of the world we have made an impregnable citadel for our Fuhrer."

The documentary claimed that the Nazis set up a base under the ice of Antarctica and by 1939 they were making regular trips with mining and tunneling equipment, and personnel including scientists, engineers and workers.

It was this base that Admiral Byrd and Operation Highjump were supposedly charged with destroying. Byrd's armada included a carrier, the USS Philippine Sea, twelve sub-carriers, a sub, about two dozen carrier-based aircraft and 4,700 personnel.

On February 26, 1947, the expedition was met with fierce resistance in the form of flying saucers that emerged from the water and attacked them. The saucers shot some type of ray, sinking a destroyer, downing about half the carrier-based aircraft and killing dozens of men. Then after the attack the saucers dove back into the water.

The operation was scheduled to last for six months, but was terminated in just two, in defeat and retreat. The Soviet report claimed Byrd reported to commission investigating officers, "in the event of another war, America can be attacked by an enemy that has the ability to fly from pole to pole with incredible speed."

Byrd gave an interview to the Argentine press before he was later muzzled by Washington.

Many insider testimonies gathered over the years have claimed, the existence of joint Nazi/extraterrestrial bases hidden under the ice of Antarctica. These reports also claim that Admiral Byrd was sent to Antarctica to negotiate with the Nazis the year before Operation Highjump, but failed to achieve any agreement.

If it's true that Admiral Byrd's armada was defeated by a squadron of flying saucers able to exit and enter from the ocean at will, then we can surmise that these were indeed alien aircraft. The Nazis did have a flying disk development program, but at no time did they ever reach that level of ability.

In a posthumously-released diary attributed to Admiral Byrd, he claimed to have had a meeting with Nordic aliens at the North Pole. This meeting was supposed to have happened in February of 1947, the same time frame that Byrd was supposed to be getting his butt kicked in Antarctica. We believe this meeting may really have taken place, but that Byrd changed the location from the South Pole to the North Pole. [40]

Byrd claimed to have flown his plane into an artificially-lit, temperature-controlled, huge underground cavern. According to the diary, during his flight Byrd's compasses began to "gyrate." His plane entered a weird valley with green grass where he saw a living wooly mammoth, a forest and a crystal city in the distance. He could no longer see the sun and his exterior temperature gauge read seventy four degrees Fahrenheit.

His radio wasn't working when he tried to report to his base camp, but then a voice with a slight "Nordic or Germanic accent" came over the radio to tell him his plane would be safely landed for him. He was then flanked by aircraft bearing swastikas. At this point he had no more control of his plane and it landed by itself.

He was taken to meet an elderly man called the "master," who gave him a message to take back to "the powers of your world," essentially warning the human race to stop using nuclear weapons, and assuring us they would preserve our species and somehow safeguard us from complete annihilation. Though his message conveyed a dire warning, the master was warm and friendly to Byrd calling him "my son" several times.

In an excerpt from the diary the master greets Byrd and confirms that he is in an underground location, "I bid you welcome to our domain, Admiral. I see a man with delicate features and with the etching of years upon his face…You are in the domain of the Arianni, the inner world of the Earth."

In another part of the message, the master confirms that they usually stay out of our race's business. "We have never interfered before in your race's wars, and barbarity, but now we must, for you have learned to tamper with a certain power that is not for man, namely, that of atomic energy."

He then confirms their race has made contact with our government to no avail. "Our emissaries have already delivered messages to the powers of your world, and yet they do not heed. Now you have been chosen to be witness here that our world does exist. You see, our culture and science are many thousands of years beyond your race."

Then the master promised to keep our race safe from annihilation. "The dark ages that will come now for your race will cover the Earth like a pall, but I believe that some of your race will live through the storm… We see at a great distance a new world stirring from the ruins of your race, seeking its lost and legendary treasures, and they will be here, my son, safe in our keeping. When that time arrives, we shall come forward again to help revive your culture and your race."

Doesn't this sound warm and fuzzy? They are going to protect us from ourselves. They will preserve some of our race, keeping us safe from ourselves. How very sweet.

However, the people dragged screaming from their beds in the middle of the night, taken to ships and having experiments performed on them while they are paralyzed might not think it's so sweet. We think they are much less likely to appreciate the fatherly benevolence of the master and his people, who have confirmed they are a different race, living underground, contacting us with their ships and abducting us at their pleasure; supposedly for our benefit.

Byrd relayed his message in a staff meeting at the Pentagon and the president (Truman) was advised. He was then debriefed by security and medical staff and ordered to remain silent about his ordeal. He complied with the order until near the end of his life when he felt compelled to tell his story.

Byrd was a national hero of unimpeachable character. This account aligns with our belief that these flying UFOs in our airspace are launched from vast underground bases; it explains why UFOs seem to be so particularly interested in nuclear facilities and shines a light on the possible motive for alien abductions.

The release of this diary lent credence to the "Hollow Earth" theory, a particularly crazy supposition that says the whole Earth is hollow and there is a sun in the middle and people live upside down on the bottom of the Earth's crust inside the planet.

We in no way subscribe to this interpretation of Byrd's diary, nor to this theory. We do NOT think the whole Earth is hollow, nor do we think there is a sun inside it.

We do believe that large caverns have been hollowed out and there are separate races living in them that are preying on us and on our livestock. But, they don't live upside down on the bottom of the Earth's crust, and their light and warmth come from their superior technology and not a sun inside our planet.

CHAPTER FOUR

MYTHS OF
UNDERGROUND CIVILIZATIONS

In ancient Irish mythology we find stories of a race of beings called the Tuatha Dé Danann (Tribes of the Gods). They were also called the shining ones. They were said to be tall, luminous magicians of giant stature; they had superior, yet ancient knowledge in the deep past of British Isles' lore. They were the elite, the builders and the priestly caste, the possessors of magic weapons, with conduits to the divine. They were said to be red-haired with green or blue eyes.

Wikipedia says they "...are often depicted as kings, queens, Druids, bards, warriors, heroes, healers and craftsmen who have supernatural powers. They dwell in the Otherworld but interact with humans and the human world." [80] [81] [82] [83]

These people were said to be the ancestors of the fairy folk of Irish mythology. Irish fairy folk are not like our familiar Tinkerbell-type of fairy. They are called the sídhe (pronounced she) and they are a fickle and unpredictable race of beings that frequently abduct humans who venture into their fairy rings. [83]

Ancient texts sometimes described the Tuath Dé as fallen angels who were neither wholly good nor evil.

They were said to have arrived in airships, landing on a mountain, and legends claim they retreated deep underground.

They were said to travel in balls of light.

They remained forever young.

They would kidnap people taking them to their realm, sometimes returning them many years later.

According to Morgynbard.com, "From Gaelic mythology comes the Four Treasures of the Tuatha Dé Danann…or the 'Tribe of Danu,' which tells us they are a tribe of divine beings, who came to Ireland after learning sacred knowledge, mystical arts and magical skills in the 'north of the world.' Some accounts say they arrived in Ireland in clouds of mist, others say they arrived on ships and burnt them to prevent retreat, with the resulting smoke becoming the 'mist.'

The Tuatha Dé Danann brought the Four Treasures with them from four magical 'cities' of Findias, Gorias, Murias and Falias. The treasures are the Sword of Nuada, the Spear of Lugh, the Cauldron of the Dagda, and the Lia Fáil (Stone of Destiny).... Each of the treasures is named after a prominent deity of the Tuatha Dé Danann. The Dagda is an earthy father-figure, both a provider and guardian, associated with abundance, generosity, regeneration and the change of seasons. Nuada is a king and wise leader, able to discern truths and engage the burdens of responsibility with honesty and courage. Lugh is a youthful champion of the tribe and master of many skills." [80]

One of their names, "Tribe of Danu," may link the beings with the Sumerian god Anu. Anu is also the name of the mother of the Irish gods.

They are said to be connected to the Druids, who were also holders of knowledge and wielders of magic.

In 1,700 B.C. the Milesians, who came from Iberia, attacked Ireland led by a Druid named Amergin seeking revenge for the death of his great-uncle, killed by the Tuatha Dé Danann. The result of this war was a truce. The Milesians would live on the surface world of Ireland and the Tuatha Dé Danann retreated underground through the gateways of the Irish earthen mounds.

They were said to have eventually evolved into elf-like creatures. Sometimes lights are seen in the fairy rings on the mounds and when this happens, humans can go into the light and visit the fairy world. [82]

We wonder if these beings could be the Nordic aliens, and the "elves" they are supposed to have evolved into might be the Greys.

OTHER HOLLOW MOUNTAINS

According to Wikipedia, "California's Mount Shasta has been the subject of an unusually large number of myths and legends. There are stories of giants, bigfoots, strange disappearances, star people and underground civilizations. In particular, it is often said to hide a secret city beneath its peaks. In some stories, the city is no longer inhabited, while in others, it is inhabited by a technologically advanced society of human beings or mythical creatures." These people were said to have taken refuge in Mount Shasta to survive some kind of cataclysm. [84]

One of the local Native American tribes, the Klamath people, believed humans originated from Mount Shasta, that people emerged from it and then populated the world.

People have reported alien encounters on and around Mount Shasta. There is a huge underground lava tube network in the area called Pluto's Cave which is said to be the site where several alien encounters have taken place with human-looking aliens.

A mining engineer, Guy Warren Ballard, was surveying Mount Shasta in 1930. He claimed to have encountered a mysterious glowing being dressed in white who he called the Ascended Master, and who was later known to him as Saint Germain. He said the being taught him the secrets of enlightenment. [85]

The mountain is located on a ley line and has a huge negative magnetic anomaly around it studied and reported on by Oregon State University. [86]

THE ALIEN GARAGE

There is a mountain in France, Mount Bugarach, which is famous for UFO sightings. The mountain has a large network of limestone caves threading throughout it. Locals believe it to be an alien base that has existed for thousands of years. [87]

In December of 2012, a large group of new age believers descended on the town believing the aliens who reside inside the mountain would save them from the imminent Mayan apocalypse.

From an article about the event: "With a steady stream of almost 20,000 visitors per year, alien-scientists and fanatics alike have come to the foot of the mountain, or alien garage as they like to call it." [88]

ITALY'S MYSTERIOUS MOUNTAIN

Mount Musine is another area with UFO activity that's been taking place for thousands of years. UFO sightings number in the thousands and there are rumors the mountain is another hollowed-out alien base. The mountain is an inactive volcano about twenty kilometers from Turin, Italy. The mountain is located along a ley line called the Saint Michael Line and like Mount Shasta is in the middle of a magnetic energy vortex. [87]

There are many stories of bizarre disappearances, portals and abductions.

Any inactive volcano has a throat that once reached through the Earth's crust into the mantle. UFOs are frequently seen emerging from volcanoes, which may be easy corridors into deep underground bases.

The area around Mount Musine was populated by Celtic tribes going back to the Neolithic age so there may be connections to the Tuatha Dé Danann. There are petroglyphs in the area depicting Cernunnos, the horned god of the Celts, and others that show human-like beings wearing what appear to be glass helmets.

There is a very weird story involving two hikers in an incident that took place on December 8, 1978. They were overwhelmed by an intense, blinding light coming from the top of the mountain. Then one of the hikers disappeared right in front of the other. The one who disappeared was found hours later, in shock and with a severe burn on the leg. He claimed to have been paralyzed and lifted by four aliens who'd descended from a ship. Months later, the two hikers suffered from a rare, acute form of conjunctivitis. [89]

THE ANT PEOPLE OF THE HOPI

An article by Gary David describes the Ant People of the Hopi, a Native American tribe of Northern Arizona. The Ant People were instrumental in saving the Hopi people from two terrible cataclysms. The first time was destruction by fire and the second destruction by ice.

During both catastrophes, "the virtuous members of the Hopi tribe were guided by an odd-shaped cloud during the day and a moving star at night that led them to the sky god named Sotuknang, who finally took them to the Ant People — in Hopi, Anu Sinom. The Ant People then escorted the Hopi into subterranean caves where they found refuge and sustenance.

Again we see a possible connection to the god Anu in the Hopi name.[90]

A book by David makes many connections between the Ant People and the gods of Babylonia and Egypt and their mutual reverence for the constellation Orion: "It is interesting to note that the Babylonian sky god was named Anu. The Hopi word for 'ant' is also anu, and the Hopi root word naki means 'friends.' Thus, the Hopi Anu-naki, or 'ant friends,' may have been the same as the Sumerian Anunnaki—the beings who once came to Earth from the heavens." [91]

Hopi petroglyphs show the Ant People to be very tall beings with large eyes and two antennae. These images are reminiscent of the Sumerian statues showing the Anunnaki with huge eyes.

They are described as generous, benevolent and industrious. They were the teachers of the Hopi, giving them the skills of proper food storage and underground bean sprouting.

This statue is thought to be of the god Anu. It has been dated to the 3rd millennium B.C.; nearly 5,000 years old. This piece is one of several depictions of the Anunnaki shown with these huge, staring eyes. Drawing by Leslie Shaw.

ANCIENT STORIES OF UNDERGROUND WORLDS

An ancient Jewish text called the Zohar relates stories of six additional realms inside the Earth, subterranean, one below the next. It is also said they are inhabited by other intelligent hybrid beings that are half human. These beings are supposed to be very different from the humans on the surface, sometimes described as having big black eyes and tiny noses. Many cultures have stories about previous ages of technological advancement that are somehow laid low by various different cataclysms.[92]

The ancient Vishnu Purana text of India describes multiple underground worlds believed to be inhabited by intelligent creatures. [92]

There are many strange stories of inhuman encounters taking place in deep caves. Sometimes these beings impart teachings and wisdom. Sometimes they are described as scaled humanoids. [92]

The hidden kingdom of Shambhala is said to be near Mount Kailash, Tibet. It is said to be an underground realm of the gods with kings that live hundreds of years. [92]

Hopefully the reader has gleaned an understanding of the answer to the "where are so many UFOs coming from" question. We believe they are hiding and being launched from underground bases. There are also reported sightings of very large UFOs with the ability to cloak themselves. There is the possibility that some of these people are residing for the long term in these kinds of ships, frequently referred to as "motherships." But the place they are hiding ON our planet, is IN our planet.

Billionaire and UFO investigator Robert Bigelow once said in an interview, "aliens are already here on Earth right under people's noses." [93]

We believe he meant this literally and his "under people's noses" comment referred to underground alien bases.

If alien bases really exist, Bigelow is a prime candidate to be in the know about them. He was a hotel magnate who founded Bigelow

Aerospace, a company that designed expandable space habitats, and the National Institute for Discovery Science, a paranormal research organization. Bigelow Aerospace is one of the corporations that supposedly received alien technology for commercial development projects.

He was the owner of Skinwalker Ranch and he spent many millions of dollars researching the strange phenomena there. [94]

CHAPTER FIVE
THE GREAT FLOOD

Why are they hiding underground? If they made the decision to install themselves in underground cities and bases, why did they do so?

We will now explore the possible reasons why an advanced civilization might choose to reside underground.

The Great Flood really happened and irrefutable proof has finally been found.

Some believe the proof was always there in the form of flood stories in the ancient myths of hundreds of cultures worldwide. Most of us know about a few of these flood myths, but in the book *The Great Flood: A Handbook of World Flood Myths*, Sir James G. Frazer researched hundreds of these stories. This book provides compelling evidence indicating a great, worldwide flood really did occur. His research found about five hundred separate cultures of peoples from around the globe who all had a flood myth in their oldest lore. Since his work was written, further study has raised that number to almost 1,200 cultures. [95]

With so many flood stories, so similar in detail, spread so widely around the entire planet, it points to a common, shared event that took place in our ancient past that affected all the people of the Earth. [99]

We are all familiar with the story of Noah's Ark told in the book of Genesis in the Old Testament.

This Great Flood illustration, called "The Deluge" was published in "Bible books of new testament and old testament (1875) scan by Ivan Burmistrov."

In the story, Yahweh, the God of Israel, warns Noah that he is going to destroy the world. Noah is told by God to build an ark and fill it with people and animals. God tells him that he is angry with man and regrets making us. He is going to destroy humanity, but is giving Noah a warning and a chance to escape the fate of his wicked contemporaries. He chooses Noah and his family to perpetuate the human race. [96]

Wikipedia says, "A flood myth, or deluge myth, is a myth in which a great flood, usually sent by a deity or deities, destroys civilization, often in an act of divine retribution." Frequently the flood destroys a bad, unruly race of men to be replaced by a more pious, God-worshiping people.

There are hundreds of flood myths that are less well-known to us Westerners. What follows is a few of these examples: [97]

China calls their mythical flood the Gun-Yu, which lasted for generations causing storms and famine. [97]

The Egyptian flood myth tells how humanity began plotting against the god Ra, who called the gods into council to decide what to do. He decided to set the lion goddess Sekhmet on the humans. She unleashed her fury on the miscreant children, and her wrath was so terrible that Ra relented and decided he must put a stop to her. He flooded all the fields of Egypt with beer; Sekhmet was attracted by the beer and drank so much that she became drunk and passed out. A few humans were thus saved and able to begin a new life. [97]

In a Maya flood myth, the Popol Vuh, the creator gods tried three times to create a god-worshiping people, before destroying these creations and making humans. [97]

The Egyptians speak of a great flood in the Edfu Building Texts, which talks about the island of the primeval one that is destroyed by a flood. The survivors then moved their civilization to Egypt. [98]

The Inca flood story is called Unu Pachakuti. In it, Virachocha caused the flood to destroy the people, saving only a man and woman to bring civilization back to the world. They floated to Lake Titicaca in a wooden box. [97]

In another Inca story the supreme god, Con Tici, first created a race of giants who became unruly. They were destroyed by a flood and turned to stone. After the deluge, God created human beings from smaller stones.[97]

The Greeks recount a tale in the myth of Deucalion about the insolence and general terrible behavior of mankind and the wrath of God in, *Washing Pre-Modern Man from the Earth's face.* God spared Deucalion and his family and also instructed him to ensconce himself, his wives, children and many different animals in a "coffer." [97]

Plato also relates a story of how Zeus decided to destroy the world. The people of Hierapolis speak of a "great chasm" opening (apparently when Zeus felt some compassion at the end) and the flood waters draining. To this day, a ceremony still occurs to honor this event. [99]

The Native American Cree people tell how many centuries ago a great flood covered the Earth, destroying all the nations. While the people were all drowning, a young virgin named K-wap-tah-w grabbed the foot of a very large bird, which carried her up to a high cliff, safely above the flood waters. Here the girl had twins fathered by the war-eagle. From those twins the world was repopulated. [97]

The Native American Hopi people tell how Tawa, the sun spirit, destroyed the Third World in a great flood. Before the destruction, Spider Grandmother sealed the more righteous people into hollow reeds which were used as boats and escaped to a small piece of dry land. Spider Woman then told the people to make boats out of more reeds, and the people sailed east until they arrived on the coasts of the Fourth World. [97]

The Inuit, or Eskimo, people tell how a great inundation, together with an earthquake, swept the land so rapidly that only a few people escaped in their skin canoes to the tops of the highest mountains. [97]

The Malaysian Temuan people tell how thousands of years ago, many people died because they had committed sins that angered God and their ancestors. God sent a punishment in the form of a great flood which had drowned all the sinners. Only two Temuans, named Mamak and Inak Bungsuk, survived by climbing on an eaglewood tree. [97]

Thailand has a myth that says the descendants of the first man and woman were wicked and crude as well as not interested in worshiping the supreme god. The god got angry and punished them with a great flood. Fortunately, some descendants survived because they fled into an enormous magical gourd. [97]

Another famous flood myth is the Ragnarok told by the Norse people. It describes a fiery conflagration followed by a flood and a long period where clouds cover the sky and the Earth turns to ice. [97]

In the Vedic texts of ancient India, a legend tells of King Manu and how he was warned about an imminent flood by Vishnu in the form of a fish. The king built a great boat and survived.

An ancient Sumerian poem called *The Epic of Gilgamesh* tells how the god Ea sent a flood to wipe out all humanity except for Utnapishtim, also called Ziusudra, and his family, whom Ea warned in advance. After the flood, the god Enlil forgave Utnapishtim. [97]

In a Korean folktale, a boy who was the son of a tree and a fairy rode on his father during a great flood. In it he rescued animals, then married and became the progenitor of humanity.

In the Philippines, the story of Ifugao says the river gods became angry and overflowed their banks, wiping out all of humanity except for two survivors who repopulated the earth after the water receded. [97]

The list of flood myths goes on and on, but most of them have two important things in common.

One is the people are warned in advance that a terrible, destructive, cataclysmic flood is coming and they are told to either get to high ground or build a boat, ship or ark in order to survive.

And two, after the flood waters recede and human civilization is in ruins, descending back into barbarism and in some cases cannibalism, a god-like teacher arrives to help guide them back towards civilization.

There is further proof that the world experienced a period of cataclysmic destruction. There is a puzzling lack of diversity in the DNA of the human population. Genetic researchers have determined that at sometime in our past, the number of human beings was drastically reduced into a population bottleneck of several thousand individuals from whom we repopulated the earth.

CHAPTER SIX

A SMALL
EXTINCTION EVENT

More proof of the Great Flood and of the Ragnarok's "fiery conflagration" comes by examination of the Usselo Horizon, a charcoal-rich deposit layer of soil found in over ten countries across Europe, Africa, India, North America and Australia.

It was discovered by Dutch archaeologist Cornelis Hijszeler in 1940 in a Netherlands sandpit at Usselo near Enschede.

Johán B. Kloosterman spoke about just how widespread Hijszeler's discovery is in the manifesto, "The Usselo Horizon, a Worldwide Charcoal-Rich Layer of the Alleröd Age."

In his manifesto, Kloosterman dates the horizon to between 11,000 and 13,000 years ago. This rich deposit of ash proves the earth experienced a widespread fiery conflagration near the end of the last ice age. [100]

About 35,000 years ago our planet was just beginning to emerge from an ice age. Over the next twenty thousand years the Earth became warmer and warmer and the ice sheets significantly withdrew.

Then about 13,000 years ago this progress to a warmer world was suddenly halted and reversed, and for the next 1,100 years, the planet was plunged back into a temporary ice age with violent, deadly weather patterns, eerily similar to the description of the Ragnarok in Norse legend, where clouds covered the sky and the sun itself became a myth that few believed.

There is a layer of soil corresponding to this period referred to as the Younger Dryas Barrier or Boundary, immediately above and laid down after the Usselo Horizon; ending about 1,100 hundred years later.

For many decades scientists have been looking for the cause of the extinction event that happened roughly 13,000 thousand years ago at the end of the last ice age. In a very short time, dozens of species all died out very quickly and at almost the same time. North America lost many of its plains (low-ground) animals, the saber-toothed cat, the mastodon, the wooly mammoth, the American horse, a giant armadillo-like creature called a glyptodon, the short-faced bear (described as a grizzly bear on stilts), the dire wolf, the American cheetah, the giant beaver, the American camel and the mammoth ground sloth, just to name a few. Another mysterious extinction, also coinciding with this time period, is the disappearance of the Clovis people of North America. [101]

A massive, devastating flood had to be considered as a possible explanation for these disappearances.

The modern-day animals that currently occupy the plains area of North America are animals that also reside at high elevations in our mountains. It is these animals that could have repopulated the plains after the flood, with a drastically reduced level of diversity than prior to the cataclysm.

Everyone who has visited Yellowstone National Park knows that bison reside there. As the white man moved across the plains of our country, they reported herds in the millions. A flood could have devastated the population of all the plains animals, opening up the habitat to be filled by the bison and the pronghorn antelope (also found at high elevations), but wiping out the other larger animals of the plains.

Early theories on the loss of the wooly mammoth included the ludicrous idea that mankind hunted them to extinction. Even if this were true (it isn't), then what happened to all the other animals lost to this time? Science continued to seek a more rational explanation.

Some scientists surmised that a meteor or asteroid impact had caused both the climate change evidenced by the Younger Dryas Boundary and the extinction event and might be the source of so many worldwide flood stories.

Nanodiamonds, also called micro beads, were found in the Usselo Horizon and the Younger Dryas Boundary, proving the cause of the boundary to be the impact of a celestial object. These particular types of diamond form ONLY in these kinds of impacts. Nanodiamonds form when a celestial body falls at very high speed through our atmosphere, bringing dust particles with it. These dust particles become superheated and form into tiny little round diamonds. The presence of these diamonds were incontrovertible proof that a meteor was the cause of the Younger Dryas Boundary and caused the climate disruptions that began 13,000 years ago.

Finding nanodiamonds in the Younger Dryas Boundary was indeed the smoking gun, proving once and for all that a celestial body slammed into the earth around 13,000 years ago. As soon as these nanodiamonds were discovered, it was all over except for the shouting. When we refer to the "shouting" here, what we mean is the debate of mainstream academia when exposed to new evidence.

The "shouting" in this case droned on and on for decades with no large public notification or acceptance. There was no announcement on the nightly news saying, "Scientists agree that the mass extinction event of 13,000 years ago was likely caused by a meteor or asteroid strike," or, "Scientists agree that the flood myths in all our cultures were likely the result of a real worldwide flood brought about by a meteor or asteroid impact." Instead, this is what happens in mainstream academia. If there is new evidence or a new idea presented, no matter how definitive the proof, it can be bandied about for years and frequently the result is to be mostly ignored.

One group of scholars was busy not ignoring the nanodiamond proof; they were devoting time to its study.

According to a study published in the *Journal of Geology* by James Kennett, a professor emeritus in the Department of Earth Science at the University of California, Santa Barbara, a team of international scientists found a very large quantity of tiny nanodiamonds distributed over millions of square miles at the Younger Dryas Boundary. Kennett found a "rich assemblage of nanodiamonds" in the Younger Dryas Boundary over three continents, but especially in North America and western Europe. [102]

Kennett also concluded that these nanodiamonds could only have been formed by "cosmic impact." [103]

In a paper "Study examines 13,000-year-old nanodiamonds from multiple locations across three continents," by Julie Cohen also at UC Santa Barbara, Cohen bases many pertinent conclusions drawn from her assessment of Kennett's study. [104]

Cohen believes a "comet collision" played a major role in the massive extinction of the Pleistocene period and "precipitated the Younger Dryas period of global cooling close to 12,800 years ago." She concluded that this impact led to the extinction of many large animals in the Americas, to the disappearance of the "prehistoric Clovis culture" and to the subsequent "human population decline." [105] [106]

But if there was such an asteroid impact, then where was the crater? Finally, the shouting can now cease (slowly cease over the next two decades), because irrefutable evidence for an asteroid impact about 13,000 years ago has been found!

CHAPTER SEVEN

HIAWATHA IS DISCOVERED

Ironically, it was our own current climate crisis that finally proved what happened 13,000 years ago. In 2016 the Hiawatha impact crater was discovered in Greenland. The receding ice cap finally made the discovery possible. This asteroid impact was the single most significant event to happen to the human race in our long history and almost nobody knows about it. Did you know about it? No? Then you're welcome.

In July of 2016, Kurt Kjær, a geologist at the Natural History Museum of Denmark in Copenhagen, discovered the Hiawatha impact crater in the Hiawatha Glacier located in northern Greenland. News of the find was released to the world in a 2018 article by Paul Voosen in the Science Journal. [107]

In the article Voosen writes Kjær traveled to the site because he "suspected the glacier was hiding an explosive secret." During the visit Kjær, found the all-important shocked mineral crystals in a river of glacial melt draining out from beneath the glacier. These crystals were what he needed to confirm his suspicions.

Kjær's team "found glass grains forged at temperatures higher than a volcanic eruption can generate. More importantly, he discovered shocked crystals of quartz. The crystals contained a distinctive banded pattern that can be formed only in the intense pressures of extraterrestrial impacts or nuclear weapons."

Kjær had discovered the thirty-one-kilometer-wide Hiawatha impact crater, a circle large enough to contain Washington, D.C.

In a later report authored by Kjær and twenty co-authors, the size of the Hiawatha Asteroid is described as one and a half kilometers in diameter, one of the "twenty-five largest known craters in the world." Though the timing was still under debate at the time of the report, some of the researchers surmised that the impact occurred roughly 13,000 years ago, "just as the world was thawing from the last ice age." By now that time period will be sounding very familiar.

Ground penetrating radar found a raised area in the center of the crater where the ground rebounded. This kind of rebounding is only formed by impacts of celestial bodies or atomic weapons. [108]

THIS IS IT! THIS is the impact that scorched the earth creating the Usselo Horizon, that vaporized billions of tons of ice in a matter of seconds, saturating the atmosphere with too much water to hold, causing worldwide torrential rains, leading to an influx of fresh water into the Earth's oceans, interrupting ocean currents and causing temperatures to drastically drop, covering the Earth in a cloud layer and plunging us back into the ice age from which we had been receding, all in a matter of minutes. [109]

Kjær and his team said the asteroid impact would equal "the energy of seven hundred, one-megaton nuclear bombs."

Proponents of the Younger Dryas impact now feel fully vindicated in their assertions. Kennett himself wrote, "I'd unequivocally predict that this crater is the same age as the Younger Dryas."

An impact like Hiawatha would have set the forests of North America and northern Europe on fire, creating the soot that is evidenced by the Usselo Horizon. It would have blown enormous amounts of dust into the atmosphere, blocking the light and cooling the region. The ice and dust that had risen into the sky would have fallen back down to Earth and into the oceans.

Kjær's team estimated the impact would have melted 1,500 gigatons of ice (about as much ice as Antarctica has lost because of global warming in the past decade.) "The local greenhouse effect from the released steam and the residual heat in the crater rock would have added more melt. Much of that freshwater could have ended up in the nearby Labrador Sea, a primary site pumping the Atlantic Ocean's overturning circulation," A single gigaton is one billion metric tons.

The impact would produce a wall of sleet and debris, moving outward in a ring of devastation at thousands of miles per hour, so quickly that it flash-froze Siberian mammoths with food still in their mouths and froze fruit trees so fast that fruit was still on them. Anyone who's had fruiting trees exposed to an early frost knows that trees drop their fruit in these conditions because the tree abandons its crop to conserve its resources in order to survive. The fruit does not remain on the tree. These trees would have had to have been flash frozen very quickly for there to still be fruit on them; they were.

When this colossal ice storm reached the oceans, it dumped billions of tons of freshwater ice and sleet into them, causing worldwide tsunamis estimated to be as high as 1,000 feet. Can you imagine a 1,000-foot-high wall of water moving towards the coastlines of the world? What would survive it? Damn little, that's what.

In only a few minutes all the low-lying areas of the world were swamped. The tsunami covered the eastern half of North America to the Rocky Mountains, killing everything in its path, wiping out the large animals of the plains and the Clovis people in a matter of moments.

By disrupting the circulation of the ocean's currents, the impact caused the reversal of our emergence from the ice age, plunging us back into a climate crisis that lasted 1,100 years.

All our technology was lost to this event and our people were chucked back into the Stone Age. Very little of our most ancient knowledge of ourselves extends back pre-flood. Our most ancient records, cities, constructions even if dated back to the earliest possible estimates rarely precede 12,900 years. Except for a few "impossible" megalithic structures and some equally "impossible" archaeological finds, we know almost nothing of ourselves prior to 13,000 years ago. Whatever advancements we'd made in the time between our emergence as modern man and the advent of the flood were scoured clean off the surface of our world in the cataclysmic flood and the 1,100 years of horrific, deadly climactic chaos that followed it.

So, whoever this god was, who warned all the different people around the world, he was able to predict the impact of Hiawatha far enough in advance for people to accomplish their survival preparations, like building an ark or relocating to higher ground. This implies he either had real god-like powers, or advanced enough astrophysics and astronomy knowledge to predict the path of an asteroid impact.

There is a story in an ancient Persian religious text called the *Vendidad* written by the prophet Zoroaster in Iran nearly 3,500 years ago. It relates another angle on the catastrophe myths of the past. [110][111]

Zoroastrianism is a very early monotheistic religion worshiping the god Ahura Mazda. This god is pictured as a man sticking out of a winged ring. The image is exactly the same in ancient Sumerian carvings and relief sculptures also found in the same region.

In this story, Ahura Mazda warned a young priest/king named Yima that a cataclysmic crisis was going to take place: "a giant serpent would descend from the heavens to the Earth and a winter would come such as has never been known."

Yima was given detailed instructions on how to build a huge underground city so that some of his people would survive the great freeze to come.

This story sounds very much like a meteor descending to Earth and also very much like the long-term climate disruption of the Younger Dryas Boundary.

Yima was instructed to bring two of every animal below ground and to construct a seed bank that would be needed after the people emerged from the life-saving underground ark.

This story differs from most flood destruction myths in that God is not warning the people about a coming tsunami. Instead they are being warned about the long term effects of the Hiawatha impact, the regression back into an ice age from which we had been emerging.

Some scholars believe this underground city has been found. In the middle of Turkey, high on a plateau in the Central Anatolia region in a town called Derinkuyu, an underground city was discovered in 2014.

This complex of underground rooms linked together by passages descends for hundreds of feet with wells for water, vents for air and rolling stone doors that would lock into place. This city could have supported a population of thousands of people. Evidence was found of stables for livestock.

Central Anatolia is a huge, high plateau region and Derinkuyu is located at an elevation of 4,200 feet. This city is at a high enough elevation and far enough inland to have perhaps been safe from a giant tsunami. It would have been an excellent location to construct an underground ark, capable of supporting its people for a very long time. [112]

So, here we have another example of a god warning people far enough in advance for them to build an underground city and make all the preparations necessary to survive the cataclysm. This particular warning would have had to come pretty far in advance to give Yima time enough to carve out an underground city; possibly years in advance.

We believe these are the people who created the site at Gobekli Tepe on the slopes of Mount Ararat. It is only 300 miles away from the underground city. This amazing site is dated to about 12,000 years ago. We believe that the people of Derinkuyu created it in thanks to their god who warned them of the disaster and gave them the plan needed to survive and the time they needed to execute the plan. The Gobekli Tepe site is made up of ringed walls built in perfect circles with giant nineteen-foot-tall, fifteen-ton, "T" shaped-stone megalithic columns. The columns are covered with designs of animals and giant relief carvings of stylized, human-like creatures that look like gods.

Nobody lived at this site; it was not a used, residential location.

One of the most bizarre things about the site is that it appears to have been deliberately buried after it was built, as if the builders wanted it to remain hidden and undefiled by time or intent. [113] [114]

There is another ancient underground city found in what is now modern-day Turkey, also on the Anatolian Plateau. It is called the ancient city of Cappadocia. The underground complex covers 100 square miles. [112]

This city is believed to have been constructed by the Hittites, 3,000 to 4,000 years ago, to protect the people from their enemies. We believe they were dug before the Great Flood and repurposed in later centuries.

The soil of the area is soft volcanic rock, perfect for tunneling.

This region is also famous for frequent UFO sightings that have been taking place for thousands of years.

CHAPTER EIGHT

HOW MANY TIMES HAS IT HAPPENED?

Is the Great Flood the first time mankind was laid low? The answer is no. It may not even be the first Great Flood.

Meteor strikes have been bedeviling mankind since the beginning of our existence. Some of them strike the land, some the ocean and in the case of Hiawatha, the ice sheet.

Here are some examples found on the Space.com website: [115]

The Barringer Crater was made when a meteor struck Arizona about 50,000 years ago.

The Lonar Crater was made when a meteor struck India between 35,000 and 50,000 years ago.

The Wolfe Creek Crater was made when a meteor struck North West Australia between 120,000 and 300,000 years ago.

The Kaali Crater was made when a meteor struck an Estonian island between 2,420 and 8,400 years ago.

The Tswaing Crater formed when a meteor struck South Africa 220,000 years ago.

The Tenolimar Crater of Mauritania, in the western Sahara Desert, is believed to have struck between 9,700 and 21,400 years ago.

These are just a few examples of land impacts. There are more from other source data. Wikipedia lists others. [116]

There is the Australasian strewn field event in Asia from about 800,000 years ago. This impact was actually linked to a Homo erectus population.

The Rio Cuarto Craters in Argentina were formed about 10,000 years ago.

A group of iron meteorites were found at Campo del Cielo also in Argentina which were estimated to be four and five thousand years old.

There are the Henbury Craters in Australia dated to about five thousand years ago.

The Whitecourt Crater in Alberta, Canada, is about 1,100 years old.

The Ch'ing-yang meteor-shower event in China happened in 1490 and reportedly killed 10,000 people.

The Kamil Crater in the southwest corner of Egypt formed about 3,500 years ago.

The Tunguska event in 1908 in Siberia, Russia, flattened an enormous forest.

This list doesn't include bolide events where small asteroids disintegrate in earth's atmosphere, but can still explode with enough force to kill, nor does it include any of the oceanic impacts.

A meteor impact crater, eighteen miles in diameter, was found in the Indian Ocean in 12,500 feet of water. Scientists believe its impact was about five thousand years ago and surmise it would have created a six-hundred-foot-high tsunami. This impact could in fact be the source of some of the flood myths in this region of the planet. [117]

The Eltanin impact hit near the tip of South America about 2.5 million years ago in about three miles of water, causing a huge tsunami, hundreds of feet high and was possibly the trigger for the ice age of the late Pliocene era. [115]

Many of these impact events could have affected the populations of humans or protohumans during their various stages of development. If at some point in our long history we reached a level of technology capable of advanced prediction of an impending asteroid impact, they could have moved a portion of their population into an underground sanctuary. Once an underground sanctuary was established, it can be surmised that a portion of that population may have chosen to remain below ground to remain safe from future surface catastrophes.

The story of Atlantis has been blown out of proportion over the years (literally). It grew from the story of a highly advanced city destroyed by a tsunami into an entire lost continent that sank into the ocean. Plato's description is of a city though. It was supposed to have existed nine thousand years before Plato's time and it was near the Pillars of Hercules, the ancient name of the Rock of Gibraltar, not a continent out in the ocean. The confusion comes because Plato talks about the city as being an island, but it's not an island out in the ocean; it's in a river delta. It's supposed to be made up of concentric rings and canals connected to each other and to the mainland by bridges.

In November of 2018, Bruce Blackburn, the CEO of an English company called Merlin Burrow, claimed to have found a site with concentric rings underwater in a bird sanctuary known as Spain's Doñana National Park. It's situated in a marsh in the mouth of a river delta just northwest of Gibraltar.

On the ocean floor, just outside the delta, is a huge pile of rubble made up of carved stones that look exactly like the kind of debris you would get if a giant tsunami pulled a stone city out into the ocean.

Blackburn believes he has found Atlantis, and we agree that he might be right. For one thing, it's in the right place.

Nobody is going to allow this guy to dig up a bird sanctuary, so this discovery may have to remain unproven, but one thing is for sure, if Atlantis existed prior to the impact of the Hiawatha asteriod, and if it was in this location along the Atlantic Ocean, it would have been devastated by the resulting tsunami. [118]

Another possible consequence of the Hiawatha impact could have been a lithospheric shift.

People think of the Earth's crust beneath their feet as fixed and stable, but it is really a thin layer of solid earth floating on a liquid layer of magma called the mantle, and a theory proposed by Harvard-educated scientist Charles Hapgood in 1958 surmises that it is possible for the earth's exterior crust to "slip" over the liquid mantle, causing a fast moving shift, which changes the Earth's two poles into new positions.

Hapgood shared his theory with Albert Einstein, who endorsed the idea. [119]

If lithospheric shifts are possible, couldn't a possible cause of them be a large asteroid crashing into the earth near the North Pole? If a lithospheric shift did occur as a result of Hiawatha's impact, it would have added to the cataclysmic chaos of the event and resulted in even higher worldwide tsunamis. It would have made the Great Flood all the more deadly and destructive.

As is evidenced by archaeological digs in Siberia unearthing mammoths and other large, extinct herbivores, Siberia used to be a grassy plain region. These animals can only be supported in a grassy plain, which comprises their food source. Siberia is now a frozen subarctic region. A lithospheric shift could be responsible for moving Siberia further north.

Hapgood's analysis was based on climate change data, changes in glacial patterns and ice ages, all pointing, in his opinion, to shifts in the positions of the poles.

Hapgood surmised that one of these shifts took place roughly 13,000 years ago, at exactly the same timeframe as the Hiawatha impact. At that time period, Hapgood believed the location of the North Pole to be along the east coast of the Hudson Bay.

Another of these shifts took place about 50,000 years ago when the North Pole was on the upper east coast of Greenland, and another about 100,000 years ago when the North Pole was in the Bering Sea.

According to Hapgood, pole shifts are times of cataclysmic chaos as oceans are ripped from their beds and tsunamis and ice ages are the result.

We believe that not only is Hapgood right in his analysis, but that the pole shift of 13,000 years ago was caused by the Hiawatha impact.

People living on the surface of our world have had to suffer terrible, regular worldwide catastrophes every time a good-size meteor struck the earth. Surface dwellers must not only suffer meteor strikes and the accompanying towering tsunamis, but a plethora of other surface-only cataclysmic problems. They have to suffer volcanic eruptions, hurricanes, tornadoes, lightning, forest fires, droughts, floods, lithospheric shifts, solar flares, earthquakes and following meteor strikes, hundreds-years-long climate change anomalies with no sunlight, failed crops and famine.

Populations living in carved-out, temperature-controlled, artificial-ly-lit caverns deep underground don't have to suffer any of these surface issues. People living in these conditions can put their energies into improving themselves and building cities that have no chance of being destroyed. They can tap into geothermal energy sources. Their crops are grown in stable, controlled environments that are never wiped out by droughts or floods.

Who saw the movie *Deep Impact*? If you did, you know what an Extinction Level Event or ELE is. For those who haven't seen the film, President Beck (Morgan Freeman) has to tell the world about a pair of asteroids that are about to crash into the Earth, killing all human and animal life on the surface.

President Beck works hard with Earth's scientists to avoid the disaster by destroying the larger of the two asteroids, which is the one large enough to cause the extinction level event. This is plan "A" to save the world.

He also lays out his plan "B" in case plan "A" fails. Plan "B" is to save what can be saved from our population, culture and very existence. The US and other world governments start building underground shelters, which he calls "arks," so our species can survive the ELE. He explains that we are going to take our brightest/best people to be the survivors, taking our knowledge and technology with them. They start choosing those who will go and those who will be left behind to die. The plan is to take our knowledge, our technology, our scientists and our healthiest athletes deep underground where they will be safe from the devastation.

Obviously this is only a movie, but many scientists give *Deep Impact* high marks in scientific plausibility.

Let us suppose for a moment that our ancestors of 13,000 years ago were technologically advanced enough to see this exact kind of disaster in their future. Mightn't they choose to do the same thing, rather than be completely destroyed?

We believe that this exact event happened before the Hiawatha impact. We were technologically advanced enough to see Hiawatha coming, so we built an ark underground with our best humans and enough surface animals to repopulate the planet with them once the flood waters receded. We did this on more than one continent so there would be several arks in different parts of the world.

After the meteor strike, when the waters receded, our people still had to contend with the returning ice age, the horrible storms and the constantly cloudy atmosphere making agriculture impossible. Instead of coming back to the surface afterward, they would have stayed below, waiting out the calamity, safe and secure in the underground ark they'd made.

If this is true, if they are really there, under our feet, then these people did NOT lose all their technology when the flood happened. They were not plunged back into the Stone Age as happened to the few surviving surface dwellers. Instead, they continued to advance, making them at LEAST 12,900 years more technologically advanced than we are.

This book explores the supposition that this is who we were before the Great Flood. In this supposition, the people buzzing our airspace might just be us. A much more technically advanced us, a possibly mutated version of us, but still us.

.

CHAPTER NINE
MEET THE TETHANS

Here, let us introduce the Tethans. They're not real; we made them up to help illustrate our point, that these people buzzing our skies in UFOs are not visiting aliens.

Let us pose a fictional scenario. Let's suppose we some day become technologically advanced enough to visit another solar system. Suppose it has an Earth-like planet with large Earth-like oceans.

On this planet, we'll call it "Tethus," after the Greek goddess married to Oceanus (why not?), we find an intelligent, but primitive race of creatures; we'll call them "Tethans."

Let's say they are bipedal like we are, but they look a little like standing dolphins with arms instead of fins. They make tools, they live in huts, they are starting to grow their own food. They have domesticated lower lifeforms they use as their main source of protein; let's call them "space cows." They are fascinating and we want to study them in great detail.

What would we do? We would probably set up a duck-blind to observe them. Maybe take a few specimens back to Earth for further study. We might leave a contingent of scientists to continue observing them. We would do our best to not interfere with them, so as not to contaminate them with knowledge about us.

What we would NOT do, is visit them 10,000 times a year every year for thousands of years. We would NOT buzz around their skies in unexplainable aircraft that would only confuse and terrify them. We would

NOT butcher their space cows for their eyes, tongues and reproductive organs, leaving the carcasses to rot in the fields. We would NOT abduct them in large numbers, taking reproductive material from them over and over again.

What possible use could aliens have for so much human DNA? Sure, they would take some samples for study, but would they abduct thousands upon thousands of people for thousands of samples, frequently abducting the same person over and over? Would they have any reason to create an alien/human hybrid breeding program?

But, what if our supposition is correct? Earth intraterrestrials might do all of these things. An advanced species of humans that has been living underground might have a very real need to abduct surface dwellers. It is possible living underground has made their population less viable. They may need regular infusions of human, surface-dwelling DNA – sperm and eggs in order to revitalize their population. They may need us as breeding stock.

As we've said before, modern ufologists report thousands upon thousands of instances of people being taken, placed on cold metal tables and experimented upon by gray-skinned humanoids with large black eyes. Frequently sperm samples are taken. Many women have reported being surgically impregnated only to have the fetuses removed at a later date. They are being used as incubators – incubators that they don't have to house or feed. These women report being taken again at a later date and allowed to see their offspring, who appear to them to be alien/human hybrids.

Humans living underground, who have no qualms about using genetic manipulation, may quickly evolve to have larger, darker eyes. They would be much paler than surface dwellers. They would only come to the surface at night because they would no longer be able to tolerate exposure to the sun. They could easily become smaller in stature.

They may be slowly evolving into the Grey alien race, or as we deem more likely, they needed a more docile and obedient race of slaves to support their society. Regular human beings make poor slaves; we strive against our captors, we revolt and fight against captivity. The Greys have frequently been described as emotionless, an excellent trait for slaves; they've retained the intelligence of a human, in fact they are probably more intelligent than we are, but without all of our inconvenient emotions and self-esteem.

And what about the other reported alien races? If you have the power of genetic engineering and no qualms about using it, why not breed Reptilians if you need them? Why not breed Bigfoots if they make stronger slave labor? Almost all reported alien sightings are of some kind of humanoid, and don't forget, Grey aliens have two nipples located in the same place as ours. These creatures, like us, evolved from lactating mammals on this planet.

We surmise that these Nordic aliens are probably the masters; "master" was the precise term given to Admiral Byrd in his meeting with the leader of the Nordic aliens.

Suppose when they went underground they took large herds of cattle and other domesticated animals with them as a food source. Those animal populations may also need regular infusions of DNA. This could explain the frequent cattle mutilations. Cattle mutilations are widespread and very consistent from one incident to another. They always take the sky-facing eye, the tongue, the blood and the reproductive organs. Always. The mutilations are always done with exacting precision and the cuts are cauterized as they are made. Something we ourselves are not capable of doing.

It is our supposition that at some point in our past, possibly right before the Great Flood or before one of the other meteor impacts, a northern European culture split off from the population and in order to survive the cataclysm retreated underground. Finding the surface of the planet to be unlivable for about 1,100 years after the flood due to climate upheavals, this population decided to remain there. At some point in time they probably realized living underground was much safer than surface dwelling. Also, 1,100 years is a long time. They may have evolved to the point that surface living became impossible, or unpalatable, causing them to abandon the prospect of returning to the surface.

Our theory is also supported by the hundreds of flood myth stories that talk about god-like teachers arriving after the flood to reeducate humans and assist in their civilization. These underground people likely were taking pity on the suffering surface dwellers. They may have felt some survivor's guilt, or were maybe motivated by their self-interest knowing they would someday need us.

Further support for this theory can be found in the actions of our government, who once they were made aware of these people, may have felt it would be in the best interest of the country to help hide evidence of them. Perhaps the underground dwellers traded dribs and drabs of their technology for aid in maintaining their secrecy and the viability of their population.

Ufology circles say that President Truman was the first president to be made aware of these people. When the upper echelons of our government discovered that we are not the most advanced people on (or in) the planet, that in fact we are very much inferior to these intraterrestrials in science and technology, they learned the intraterrestrials have a need to abduct us to continue their existence and also realized there was nothing we could do to stop them from abducting the individuals they wanted. The government may have decided to form an agreement with these people in exchange for their technology, which could be doled out to us slowly. In exchange our government would help hide the existence of these people, help cover up any of their activities, create a campaign of ridicule when surface people see them. When ridicule doesn't work, use threats, in the case of military personnel who see them, use forced and enforced non-disclosure agreements. Use punishments for those who refuse to keep quiet, even stooping to murdering the most vocal and determined of them.

We feel that this might be further proof that we are not dealing with aliens here. Would any president make such a pact with a truly alien species? We don't think so, but we believe they might do so with an advanced population of fellow humans.

We believe these intraterrestrials, these advanced humans, have been playing at being gods for thousands of years, and are now playing at being visiting alien races. Anything to distract us from the truth, that they are a subterranean branch of humans, preying on us for their needs. Why are they lying to us? We believe it is partly because of their predation upon us and also because they know that though we are not as technologically advanced as they are, we do outnumber them.

We are not the only researchers to propose this theory. In Dr. Michael E. Salla's book, *Antarctica's Hidden History,* he writes, "...as a group that the Nazis were led to believe were ET's (referred to as 'Arianni' or 'Aryans', sometimes called 'Nordics'), but were actually an ancient Earth human break-away civilization that had developed a space program (referred to as 'The Silver Fleet') and created vast bases below the Himalayan Mountains (largest in Tibet and called the system Agartha) and a few other regions."

Can you imagine the effect the finding of these Nordic "aliens" would have had on Hitler? In his mind it would have justified all his erroneous beliefs in a superior Aryan race. Conversely, the "Nordics" would have found a willing sycophant in Hitler. Is it any wonder they combined resources during World War II?

Then after the war was lost, the "Nordics" would have had to form an alliance with the remaining world powers, dangling the carrot of sharing technology in exchange for acquiescence to their culling of surface-dwelling humans and their continued anonymity. [120]

CHAPTER TEN

SO MANY IMPOSSIBLE THINGS

E vidence of a pre-flood population of technologically advanced humans comes by examining the impossible megalithic structures not
adequately explained by current academic theories. There are hundreds
of sites all over the world that exist in spite of the fact that the people
to whom they are attributed did not possess the technology necessary
to build them. Bronze-Age tools cannot even make a dent in granite,
but again and again Bronze-Age people are credited with building these
megalithic structures.

The Inca, a Bronze-Age civilization, were not equipped to haul fifty-five-ton stone blocks up goat paths to Machu Picchu. They did not
possess the ability to cut granite blocks into two-hundred-ton complex
polygonal shapes. They were not able to fit them so tightly together that a
piece of paper could not be inserted between them as is found at the walls
of Sacsayhuaman. They did not have the necessary tools to create the
layered, inward, triple beveling of the andesite stones, as hard or harder
than granite, at Puma Punku, the carving of which would be difficult to
match today with power-driven, diamond-encrusted cutting tools.

The Egyptians of five thousand years ago did not have the necessary
tools to build the Great Pyramid. While they were capable of carving
sandstone blocks, many of the stones used in the Great Pyramid and the
surrounding Giza Plateau are made of granite and diorite, stones which
are much harder than the Egyptian copper tools of the time. These giant
granite slabs were quarried 600 miles away and supposedly floated down
the Nile.

The Maya could not fly the mica used in the Pyramid of the Sun at Teotihuacan from the quarries in Brazil from which they come, roughly 2,500 miles away.

The ancient islanders of Micronesia were not capable of moving fifty-ton basalt boulders from the other side of their island in order to build the site of Nan Madol.

The trilithon stones in the base of the temple of Jupiter at Baalbek, Lebanon, weigh about 880 tons. Nobody has been able to satisfactorily explain how these stones were moved and placed on top of a twenty-foot-tall platform on top of a steep hill.

And, nobody has an explanation for the recent discoveries of underwater cities built on ground that hasn't been exposed to the air for over 12,000 years.

Pyramids all over the world show evidence of being built by the same designers, long before these cultures are supposed to have had any contact with one another. [120]

Logic dictates that at some time in our past we started out as stone-tool makers, slowly advanced to metal workers, then became builders of cities, and this took place in a straight, uninterrupted, progressive chain of events. But, this supposition just doesn't fit the facts. What actually appears to have happened is we followed this logical progression, slowly becoming builders of cities, were then laid low by a worldwide cataclysm and forced to start over at the bottom of the chain again.

We now know what the cataclysm was, it was the Hiawatha impact and the possible lithospheric shift caused by it. This is the reason evidence of our pre-flood city-making capabilities is so thin. Very few structures would have been strong enough or built high enough to have survived this impact.

Remember in Chapter 3, how most of the ancient flood myths have a god that arrives after the flood? The god comes to help the people recover from the flood; he brings knowledge and civilization back to them, teaching them not to be cannibals, how to do math and grow crops, how to build temples, etc.

The most amazing megalithic sites are frequently assumed to be constructed in the relatively recent past, because the sophistication of the architecture implies that the builders could not have been capable of building them at any earlier date. But, this is proving to be false. This assumption kind of dating was applied to the ancient megalithic city of Caral-Supe in Peru. It was decided by someone that the site could not have been constructed any earlier than two to three thousand years ago. Then some organic building material, a netted-fiber textile called quipu, was uncovered under the base of the city structure and carbon dated. To everyone's amazement, the material was dated to over five thousand years ago. This site predates the Inca civilization by three thousand years, proving once and for all that there was a megalithic-city-building civilization living in Peru thousands of years before the Inca. [122]

There are hundreds of megalithic stone structure sites worldwide that defy explanation, because they absolutely cannot have been built by the people they are attributed to. Newer theories emerging as to the age of these sites are pushing their construction further and further back in time, and it is becoming clear that the older a site is, the better it is constructed and the more impossible their construction appears to be. New theories are proving that we were technologically advanced enough before the Great Flood to build megalithic stone cities and the fierce devastation of the flood robbed us of all our collective knowledge and shoved us back into the Stone Age.

We believe that after the flood, a few of the people who went underground came back to the surface, used their superior technology and knowledge of how to build megalithic sites to construct some of these impossible places, at much earlier dates than they are currently attributed, and then returned below. As time went on, the people of the surface lost the knowledge of how to build these kinds of sites and began constructing simpler, inferior structures, with much smaller and much more sensibly-sized stone blocks. These easier constructions are built at later dates than the superior, older sites. We believe this is why many older megalithic structures are better than their later counterparts.

Some were probably built before the Hiawatha cataclysm, and others were built after the flood by those who went underground and later returned to the surface to help the survivors.

Of course this is confusing for archaeologists, who are excavating ancient sites in five-thousand-year-old soil, or much older, that are built with colossal stone blocks; blocks which are cut with perfect precision, and are STILL fitted together so tightly a toothpick can't be inserted between them, in spite of five thousand years of weathering. Also, these sites are frequently located in mountainous regions at very high elevations. We would have trouble building these cities today even using our modern machinery.

THE SITES IN PERU AND BOLIVIA

Some of the most amazing archaeological sites in the world are located in Peru and northern Bolivia. According to mainstream archeology, somehow the Inca were supposed to have built Machu Picchu, Puma Punku and the nearby complex of Tiwanaku, Sacsayhuaman, Cusco, Ollantaytambo and Caral-Supe while also somehow constructing the incredible Inca system of roads connecting all these sites all through the Andean Mountain range. All this was supposed to have been accomplished in the few hundred years the Inca empire existed and all accomplished without the wheel, draft animals or any modern tools in one of the world's steepest mountain ranges.

When the Spanish conquistadors came to Peru, they asked the Inca, "Who built these structures?" and the Inca told them that they did not build them; their ancestors did not build them. Rather, they found them as they were when their people came to the area five hundred years before. [123]

THE SITE OF TIWANAKU AND PUMA PUNKU

Tiwanaku is an enormous site next to Lake Titicaca which includes Puma Punku, a large, manmade, terraced platform mound located on a large plateau at 12,600 foot elevation, in the Andes Mountain range in Northern Bolivia, so high that it is 2,000 feet above the tree line.

Ground penetrating methods have established that the extended site is about seventeen hectares (about forty-two acres) with only two hectares exposed. Still covered by ground are two additional huge platforms. The exposed platform at the top is made up of colossal "H" blocks, weighing approximately 144 tons, made of red sandstones that come from a quarry down a steep hill about six miles away, with smaller, intricately-carved, triple-interior beveled stones made of andesite found about fifty-six miles away on the far side of Lake Titicaca.

Master stone masons of today would have to use computer-driven, diamond-tipped cutters to recreate the ninety-degree, incised-interior cuts found in the Puma Punku andesite stones. Andesite is a pretty hard rock. It is a 7 on the Moh scale; granite ranges between 6 and 7 on the scale. So andesite is at least as hard as granite. [124]

Ancient legends tell of the blocks of Puma Punku levitating into place in a single day. They say they were built by "the star people."

There doesn't appear to be a mainstream consensus on the age of the site; opinions range between 200 B.C. and 600 A.D. The people in this area during these time periods did not have the wheel and no written language, yet they were supposed to have built one of the most advanced cities of the ancient world.

The controversial engineer, scholar and colorful early explorer Arthur Posnanski (1873-1946) spent fifty years of his life in the study of ancient Andean cultures and sites, especially at Tiwanaku. He dated the site to 12,000 B.C. [125]

The triple-bevel stone cutting technique is seen here in an andesite stone at the site of Puma Punku in northern Bolivia. Andesite is a very hard stone, a 7 on the Moh scale. Granite is either 6 or 7 on the scale, so these precisely cut stones are at least as hard as granite. Modern-day stone cutters have said they would only be able to match this quality of cutting with computer-controlled, diamond-encrusted stone cutting power tools. Photo credit: iStock

The largest of the polygonal cut stones in the walls of Sacsayhuaman are estimated to be up to 200 tons. Photo credit: iStock

Archaeologists are still arguing over how these stones were transported from the lower-elevation quarry. The stone-cutting techniques were so advanced as to be considered impossible by the Inca people to whom they are attributed. The giant stones were interlocked with each other, the perfect precision of the angles of the interior bevel cuts into the andesite stones and perfectly fitted joints reflects an understanding of descriptive geometry.

The blocks are all perfect copies of each other, so perfect they would be interchangeable. The uniformity of these blocks is itself a mystery. How were these primitive people able to precisely replicate their cutting techniques from one block to the next.

SACSAYHUAMAN (THE HEAD OF THE FALCON)

This site is above the city of Cusco, Peru, at 12,142 foot elevation. It is a hilltop plaza with three large zig-zagging stone walls made from colossal blocks weighing up to two hundred tons. These stones are andesite, just like at Puma Punku, so they are a 7 on the Moh scale, much harder than the bronze tools used by the Inca. [113 123 126 127]

They are mostly polygonal shapes, with almost no two the same. There is no way the Inca could have cut these stones with their bronze tools.

The walls have no mortar, are up to six meters high and all lean inward. But, the strangest thing about them is that all of the stones are slightly rounded, as if a high-heat source had slightly melted them.They are again cut and fitted together so perfectly that nothing can be pushed between them.

Local legend says a falcon built the walls using a powerful chemical it kept in its beak, a substance that could melt stone.

Cusco, Peru, sometimes spelled "Cuzco," was the capitol of the Inca Empire and is also known for ancient megalithic construction. The site is near Sacsayhuaman. Note the complex stone cutting technique and the amazing tight-fitting seams between the stones. Photo credit: iStock.

The quarry where the stones were cut is twenty-two miles away from the site at 11,500-foot elevation. According to mainstream academia, the Inca, without the wheel or draft animals, were supposed to have dragged these two-hundred-ton stones over twenty-two miles of mountainous terrain to a site 642 feet higher than the quarry using hemp and llama skin cables and at an altitude so high that trees can't survive there. We call bullshit.

MACHU PICCHU

This site is only about 8,000 foot elevation, but it still exhibits the cyclopean-style of architecture found at Sacsayhuaman, with fifty-five-ton polygonal shaped stones. The unique impossibility of this site is how steep and precipitous the river canyon over which it is perched and also

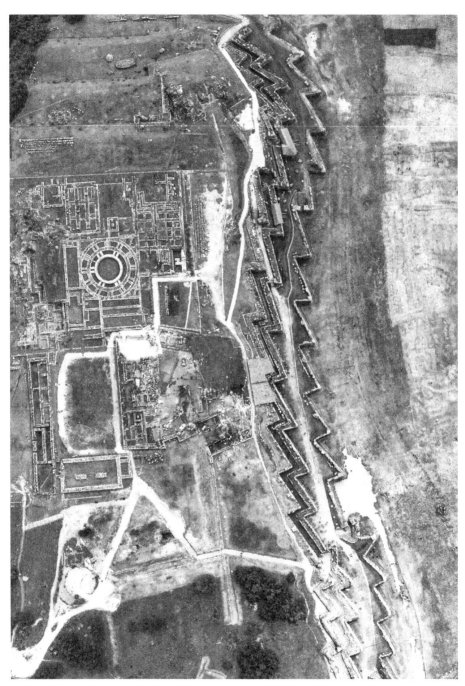

The zig-zagging walls at Sacsayhuaman only flank one side of the site. They would be useless for defense, so they must have served some other purpose. Photo credit: iStock

This view from above Sacsayhuaman shows the length of the triple-deep zig-zagging, stone walls. Photo credit: iStock

No two of the megalithic stones in the wall of Sacsayhuaman are the same, yet they fit together so tightly that a credit card can't be inserted between them. Photo credit: iStock.

how remote the location. The walls are made of granite, a 6 or 7 on the Moh scale. Just like Sacsayhuaman, the stones are slightly rounded with the same incredible tight fit using no mortar.

This site is located on two earthquake faults, but the walls have not fallen; further testimony to the fantastic engineering of the architecture.

There is no doubt that the Inca repurposed these sites. Machu Picchu, Sacsayhuaman and other sites show signs of Inca stone work on top of the older colossal-stone architecture. The Inca constructs are using much, much smaller rocks held together with mortar. Organic remains at the site which have been carbon dated are evidence of the much more recent Inca habitation. [127]

TEOTIHUACAN

The mystery of this site rivals that of the Great Pyramid in Egypt. This city is the oldest in the region, Central Mexico, yet it is the most advanced. Unlike later cities, this giant complex has no hieroglyphs, so nobody knows who built it, where they came from or who ruled there. There are ruins under the main structures that appear to exhibit even more advanced building techniques with even larger megalithic rock. For instance, the largest pyramid, the Pyramid of the Sun, is composed of five interior pyramids, each built on top of the next, and the innermost of these nested pyramids shows the most advanced engineering techniques.

The complex covers eight square miles with two hundred buildings including two very large pyramids, the Pyramid of the Sun and the Pyramid of the Moon, and there is a large temple dedicated to the feathered serpent, also known as Quetzalcoatl. There are several buildings with large, flat platforms that resemble modern-day helicopter landing pads and a long, straight avenue running down the middle of the complex called the Avenue of the Dead.

The construction is dated to the first century A.D., but we believe the megalithic construction underneath is much older.

The Aztec people have a flood myth too. They believe their people lived in five separate ages, each five thousand years long. The fourth age was supposed to end in a deluge. We believe this points to a much older culture of people than is widely believed.

When the site was discovered, it was almost entirely buried in soil and had been reclaimed by the surrounding jungle. Only about 10 percent of the complex is excavated.

This fully functioning, incredibly skilled engineering culture seems to have arrived from somewhere else. The name of this city translates to "City of the Gods." There are no precursor, practice cities in the region leading up to this fantastic complex. Local legends attribute the site to twelve gods.

An American civil engineer and researcher named Huge Harleston surmised that in the layout of Teotihuacan, the actual distance between the buildings exactly matches the relative distances between the heavenly bodies of our solar system. There is even a structure where Pluto would be, and a manmade water feature at the exact location of the asteroid belt. He also found a distant temple in the exact line of the Avenue of the Dead that represents another planet, twice as far away as Pluto, that may point to an additional, yet-to-be-discovered planet in our solar system.

If this research is correct, and the ancient people who built the site knew about the existence of Pluto and the asteroid belt, then they had access to information that was not available to modern man until over two thousand years later.

But, believe it or not, the most bizarre aspects of Teotihuacan have yet to be related. The rock mica was found In several layers of the Pyramid of the Sun, and also as a lining material in several other structures at the site. The closest known source of this mica is over 2,500 miles away in Brazil. Mica is a rock particularly well suited for the distribution of heat. In fact, in modern-day technology it's used in heat shields for the aerospace industry.

That's bizarre aspect number one. In a subterranean excavation from the Avenue of the Dead extending under the Temple of the Feathered Serpent, in one chamber archaeologist Sergio Gomez discovered a lake of liquid mercury, a highly toxic substance which required a high-heat industrial process to extract. Mercury is the first known superconductor. Nobody knows if this lake was integral to the functioning of the complex, or merely a byproduct of its function.

Bizarre aspect number three is the pyrite spheres. In another chamber off the Gomez excavation, he found hundreds of gold-looking metallic spheres which are mostly clay covered by iron pyrite. Also in the chamber are thousands of flecks of pyrite that when lit, look like a starry sky with little golden planets. Some of the material inside these spheres has defied classification and remains unknown. [129]

THE OLMECS

The Olmec people lived 3,600 years ago in a small region of modern-day southern Mexico in the state of Tabasco. They are most well known for their colossal carved heads. The heads have African features but these people were never supposed to have had any contact with the people of Africa. Why were they carving the faces of people they'd never seen? The largest are eleven feet high and weigh up to fifty tons. The impossible part comes when you realize the closest source of the basalt rock from which they are carved is over 100 miles away. The fifty-ton head weighs this much AFTER being carved down. The boulder before carving would have weighed at least sixty tons.

These heads have measurable magnetic fields which are stronger on the face part of the stones, as if the makers were able to detect these fields and adjust their carvings accordingly.

The Olmec civilization is well known for their colossal carved heads. Though the Olmecs lived in what is now modern-day Mexico, these heads have African features even though these people were never supposed to have had any contact with the people of Africa. Photo credit: iStock.

Most people associate the Olmecs with the giant heads, but these people were also builders of pyramids and temples similar to the Maya and Aztec pyramids built later. At an archaeology site known as La Venta, a complex of structures and plazas includes the Olmec's Great Pyramid. It is the oldest of the Mesoamerican pyramids, standing 110 feet high. It is aligned to the North Star, proving the Olmecs had some knowledge of astronomy. The Olmecs were the builders of the Cholula Pyramid, which is the largest pyramid by volume in the world, nearly double the volume of the Great Pyramid in Egypt. It was supposed to have taken 1,400 years to build. It was later added on to by the Toltecs and the Aztecs. [129] [130]

NAN MADOL

Nan Madol is located on the Micronesian island of Pohnpei. This bizarre city covers two hundred acres, is comprised of about 700,000 tons of building material and is made up of about ninety manmade islands connected by canals. The city appears to be sticking out of the ocean and divers have found more of these structures underwater. For some strange reason, electrical devices do not work anywhere near Nan Madol, so underwater remote-viewing drones cannot be used to determine the dimensions of the immersed part of the city.

The construction of Nan Madol is attributed to twin "sorcerers" of giant proportions, Olisihpa and Olosohpa, who founded the Saudeleur Dynasty in the year 1,100 A.D. The twins were said to be much taller than the native Pohnpeians. They were supposed to have levitated the giant stones into place with the help of a flying dragon.

According to mainstream theories, these ancient islanders somehow moved fifty-ton megalithic blocks of basalt into place by floating them on rafts around the island. This floating method was supposed to have been done on the ocean, not a calm, quiet body of water, but one with waves, swells and strong currents.

The local islanders are afraid of the site. Nobody lives there. Strange floating lights are regularly seen there and the people believe the site is cursed.

The ancient legends of the local people describe an earlier sunken city, Kanamwayso, under the current structure of Nan Madol. [123] [131]

THE TEMPLE OF JUPITER AT BAALBEK

One of the most unbelievable accomplishments of ancient megalithic site builders is almost unknown to the general public. The Temple of

Jupiter was built by Alexander the Great on top of what appears to be a much older platform of stones in a high mountainous area of Lebanon. Three of the stones in this platform are called the trilithon stones. They are enormous. Their estimated weight is 880 tons each; not pounds, not kilos but tons. [132]

The temple above the platform is a different style of building, and the platform stones appear to have much more weathering than the temple above.

This site was home to the Osirians, the Canaanites and later the Romans, but none of these people were capable of moving these giant stones from the quarry over two miles away and up a steep hill, lifting them on top of a twenty-foot-high-platform of smaller stones (smaller but still enormous), and fitting them together so perfectly and tightly that a credit card cannot be inserted between them. We would have trouble moving these stones today and we certainly couldn't move them without gouging deep crane marks into them.

Some researchers believe Baalbek is the location of "The Landing Place" referred to in the five-thousand-year-old Sumerian *Epic of Gilgamesh,* where the hero of the story, King Gilgamesh, goes to ascend to the heavens and ask the gods to make him immortal. [123]

THE UNDERWATER CITIES

During the last ice age, about 32,000 years ago, the ancient city of Dvaraka was said to have been established by Lord Vishnu, along the coast of India near the modern-day city of Dwaraka. The city was mentioned in many of the ancient Indian epic texts called Puranas, including the Mahabharata and the Vishnu Purana, written in Classic Sanskrit roughly five thousand years ago. The texts talk of Lord Vishnu building a great fortified city called Dvaraka. This city was supposed to be an ancient myth, but recently two underwater cities off the coast of India in the Gulf of Khambhat have been discovered in 125 feet of water.

During an underwater excavation by the Marine Archaeology Unit of India's National Institute of Oceanography, Indian archaeologist S.R. Rao said he thought it reasonable to assume the city was Dvaraka as described in the Mahabharata.

The Mahabharata describes the city as being swallowed up by the sea in a matter of moments. It does not describe a slow rise of ocean levels slowly swamping the city, but rather some kind of catastrophic flood.

In order to be in 125 feet of water, the city must have been built during the ice age. Human beings were not supposed to be able to construct large stone cities 32,000 years ago, yet the ruins are there.

WHO built these cities? We are not supposed to have reached this level of architectural engineering until about five thousand years ago. [132] [133]

This underwater pyramid complex was discovered off the coast of Pinar Del Rio, Cuba, in two thousand feet of water. Canadian explorer Paulina Zeilitsky was doing an underwater survey of the area and found the site in 2000 feet of water. So deep that it must have been built in the middle of an ice age for the water level to be that low, at least fifty thousand years ago. Drawing by Leslie Shaw.

In 2001 evidence of another underwater city was found off the coast of Pinar Del Rio, Cuba, in two thousand feet of water. Canadian explorer Paulina Zeilitsky was doing an underwater survey of the area and found pyramids, terraces and other structures so deep that they must have been built in the middle of an ice age for the water level to be that low, at least 50,000 years ago.

Mainstream archeology has no explanation for these finds, but THEY ARE THERE!

CHAPTER ELEVEN

MAINSTREAM ACADEMIA AND THE PSEUDOSCIENTISTS

This book relies heavily on the scientific research of many geniuses and scholars whose work has been laughed out of the halls of mainstream academia, but can be proven again and again when their evidence is examined. These scholars frequently do not find a forum for their ideas in the mainstream and they are instead relegated into the fringes of the scientific community, labeled as pseudoscientists.

But, as science progresses, excavations continue and closer examination is made of both new and old evidence, many of these "fringe scientific" discoveries are being proven correct, and more and more often, mainstream archeology is being proven to be what it is: slow to change, slow to react and slow to admit being wrong.

Once mainstream academics declare something to be true, it requires a tsunami of conflicting evidence to change their opinions. One can surmise the reason for this as being their embarrassment. They must publicly declare, "We were wrong, and now we believe this instead." Frequently the conflicting evidence is much more credible, found in much larger quantities and of much better quality; but still mainstream academia closes its collective eyes and ears, and ignores mounting conflicting evidence until the embarrassment meter slowly swings to the position of "it looks worse for us to continue ignoring this." What follows is a pile of excuses as to why they erroneously believed what they did and a grudging admission that the new information is correct.

As more and more evidence is being found out about the true age of these ancient sites, more and more evidence is being piled up on the side of so-called pseudoscience. Ever so slowly the embarrassment meter of mainstream academia is inching toward the time when they will have to start abandoning their stodgy, old, erroneous assumptions and start reassessing the new discoveries that are lying at their feet.

Frequently the scientific opinions that fill our textbooks were established in the 1800s by scientists in England, who didn't have access to the modern tools of today. No DNA testing, no radio-carbon dating, etc. But, still many of these old theories persist, as if they were chiseled into stones instead of being mere words on paper.

Also, many of these opinions were not arrived at by a consensus of agreement. Many conflicting arguments were taking place in the scientific community of the day. Sometimes more credible theories were shouted down and forgotten. Sometimes the theories that rose to the top, established as fact and printed into textbooks, were based on erroneous evidence, since proven wrong. The basis for the theories is debunked, but many times conclusions gleaned from the erroneous evidence remains in place.

But, when mainstream beliefs conflict with provable facts and incontrovertible evidence, mainstream beliefs MUST BE ABANDONED!

Nowhere than in the fields of archaeology, paleontology and anthropology is slow-to-change academic stodginess more prevalent.

Currently accepted, mainstream archaeology claims that Homo sapiens have been on our planet for about 300,000 years and the most modern version, Homo sapien sapiens, have been here for between 90,000 and 160,000 years. The earliest Homo sapien sapiens are indistinguishable from the man of today. Just give them a bath, a shave and a haircut, and you wouldn't be able to tell them apart just by looking.

So, somehow mainstream archeology believes that we sat around in caves, picking fleas off our butts, for between 85,000 and 155,000 years with little to no advancement, when suddenly, and worldwide, about five thousand years ago, we decided to start advancing into a pyramid-building, megalithic-city-constructing, Stonehenge-raising, crop-producing, calendar-creating, tech-savvy people in just a few hundred years.

This widely accepted timeline is ridiculous. Are we the type of creatures that would sit stagnant for so long? Also, this mainstream version of our evolution does not take into account the hundreds upon hundreds of discoveries that contradict this timeline.

Because Hiawatha's impact plunged us back into the Stone Age, our current level of technology is only rooted in 13,000 years of uninterrupted growth and expansion. Try and imagine what our species could have become with 155,000 years of uninterrupted advancement.

THE VICE OF VYSE

One of the most outrageous and enduring frauds perpetrated on the historic record was the dating of the Great Pyramid by Richard William Howard Vyse.

Vyse began his career as a British soldier, and was later elected to Parliament. After the election, his opponent and other candidates accused Vyse of bribery and corruption during the campaign. Allegations that were proved to be true after Vyse's death.

Then somehow this lying, corrupt charlatan of a politician, along with an engineer named John Shae Perring, was put in charge of exploring the pyramids of the Giza Plateau.

In 1836, Vyse joined the excavations of the Giza Plateau being conducted by Giovanni Battista Caviglia, who had blasted into the chamber above the King's Chamber called the stress-relieving chamber. The King's Chamber had been discovered by Nathaniel Davison in 1765. Caviglia surmised that there was another chamber above the stress-relieving chamber and confided this information to Vyse.

According to letters written by Caviglia, Vyse betrayed his confidence and had Caviglia removed from the site in order to claim the discovery for himself. This was more proof that Vyse was a lying, cheating, now traitorous snake. Certainly not the kind of man to be put in charge of such an important expedition. Above all, science needs men and women of integrity, reporting their findings honestly for history and for posterity. Instead a corrupt, back-stabbing liar was put in charge of one of the most important sites in the world.

As befitting this bombastic NOT-archaeologist, in 1837 Vyse ham-handedly used gunpowder to blast access to four upper chambers above the stress-release chamber.

Vyse perpetrated this sacrilege upon the most wonderful accomplishment of the ancient world, in order to prove the theory that the pyramid was built by the pharaoh Khufu.

After Vyse opened the upper chamber, he was disappointed in his hopes of finding the mummy of Khufu and all the trappings of gold, jewels and priceless artifacts that would be interred in an Egyptian pharaoh's tomb. In fact, the Great Pyramid was found to be completely empty of all artifacts, without a single inscription or carving found in the entire structure. Vyse himself reported this in his early notes.

Then later, Vyse claimed that he did find graffiti in the pyramid after all. After already writing that he found nothing, suddenly Vyse claimed to have found a cartouche attributing the Great Pyramid as belonging to Khufu after all.

The problem is the cartouche is written in red paint, from left to right on a repaired patch of wall (it is not known when the repair took place), when cartouches of this time period were all written from top to bottom and they are hardly ever painted, but are almost always carved into stone. This is not even a clever forgery, but for the past two centuries, Egyptologists continue to attribute this pyramid to the pharaoh Khufu and continue to claim the pyramids were built as tombs for pharaohs, even when it's obvious that the pyramid was sealed with no evidence of grave robbery.

It's so obvious that this man, embarrassed by his failure to prove his theory, forged this cartouche and perpetrated a fraud on history and posterity, blinding the scientific community to the truth about the age of the Great Pyramid.

There is further proof of this fraud on the famous Inventory Stele that says the pyramid already existed in Khufu's time.

While mainstream Egyptology has swallowed Vyse's fraud, hook, line and sinker, many others did not. [136] [137]

John Anthony West, an American author and lecturer, noticed weathering patterns on various Egyptian monuments that appeared to have been caused by water erosion. He teamed up with Boston University geologist Robert Schoch and the pair eventually released their "Sphinx Water Erosion Hypothesis." The pair studied the water erosion patterns found on the Sphinx and came to the conclusion it was constructed between ten and 12,000 years ago in a much wetter climatic period. [138]

MYSTERIES OF THE GREAT PYRAMID

People who have never studied the Great Pyramid have no idea of how amazing the structure really is. Until the construction of the Eiffel Tower, it was the tallest manmade structure in the world. It is composed of 2.3 million sandstone blocks averaging fifty tons each, the heaviest of which are seventy tons. Many of the interior chambers are constructed of granite. Granite that is not found in the area, but comes from a quarry about 600 miles away.

Egyptians of five thousand years ago were using copper tools. Copper tools, even when hardened with hammering, cannot make a dent in granite, let alone cut and shape it to the levels of precision found inside the Great Pyramid.

They did not have cranes to move the blocks. Somehow they were supposed to be able to move these blocks by rolling them on logs, up ramps and somehow putting them into place. The ramps would have had to be miles long and made from the same stone. The logs would have to be hardwoods to have a chance of supporting the weight of these blocks; hardwoods are not grown in the area. There are 2.3 million blocks in the Great Pyramid and it was supposed to have been built in twenty years. That means that the ancient Egyptians would have to place fourteen blocks per hour, every hour, at night, during the rainy season, in the high heat of summer, never stopping for twenty straight years.

The people who were supposed to have built the pyramids, also like the Inca, did not have the wheel. They didn't have pulleys; they didn't have cranes or steel.

Machinists who closely examine the granite stones at the Giza plateau are finding machine marks made by lathes and saws, but no lathes or saws have ever been found. These marks would have been made by diamond encrusted tools, but no diamonds were ever found in Egypt.

The granite surfaces are ground to perfection, perfectly flat with perfect right angles and even though they are thousands of years old, the edges are so sharp you can cut yourself on them. Only machines are capable of this kind of precision.

The Egyptians of five thousand years ago did not have machines, no lathes and no saws.

Mainstream Egyptology is STILL referring to the pyramids as tombs. THEY ARE NOT TOMBS! No body, mummy or corpse of any kind has ever been found inside an intact pyramid. Never, never, never. The ancient Egyptians always tried to HIDE their tombs. They would not have wanted to entomb themselves in the most conspicuous structures in the world. [111 136]

We instead give a great deal of credence to the new theories about the pyramids being power plants.

In his book, *The Giza Power Plant: Technologies of Ancient Egypt*, Christopher Dunn makes a compelling case for the use of pyramids as power plants. Evidence has been found of residue lining the shafts leading into the Queen's Chamber. On the northern shaft there was hydrated zinc and on the southern shaft, hydrochloric acid.

Dunn's theory points out that when these two chemicals are combined, they produce hydrogen gas. He surmised this gas would rise into the King's Chamber where the molecules could be excited by vibration to produce a microwave energy beam. The Grand Gallery would have functioned as a resonator increasing the vibration.

Dunn believes that once started and sealed, The Great Pyramid would have functioned like a microwave-generating machine for years. [139]

This theory goes a long way to explaining the presence of mica in the Pyramid of the Sun. If hydrogen gas is being utilized as a combustible fuel inside these pyramids, it could explain the need for heat shielding inside the walls.

THE ANCIENT STRUCTURES OF SARDINIA AND MALTA

The ancient megalithic stone structure builders frequently aligned their constructions to astronomical occurrences. These ancient structures are not only impossible for primitive people to have built, but the necessary knowledge of astronomy needed to make these perfect alignments would have also been beyond their abilities.

The Earth has a slight wobble in its orbit that repeats in a 26,000 year cycle. This phenomenon is called the precession of the equinoxes. The wobble causes the change of our relative positions to the constellations and can be measured by a single degree in a sixty-year period. This phenomenon was supposedly discovered by a Greek astronomer named Hipparchus in 150 B.C. when he compared the positions of stars made 150 years before by another astronomer named Timocharis.

When we say "supposedly" discovered, we say this because the knowledge of precession was known to the ancient Sumerians, so it was "rediscovered" by the Greeks thousands of years later.

An ancient race of Sardinia, Italy, known as the Nuraghe were building giant tombs, castle-like structures known as Nuraghes, monuments of single upright standing, colossal carved stones called menhirs, eight-foot-tall statues with robot-like features and huge round eyes and temples with ancient astrological alignments. All their structures were built with enormous, precisely cut basalt rocks with no motor thousands of years ago. By now this building method should be sounding familiar.

One example of an inexplicably perfect astrological alignment performed thousands of years ago is the Paulilatino, the sacred well of Santa Christina. It was built on Sardinia three thousand years ago to track celestial events. This piece of workmanship is absolutely incredible. It is built below the water table, which is a feat all its own, with unbelievable stone cutting and placing engineering skills that rival modern workmanship. The positioning of the well allows the moon to shine down on the water through a hole at the top of the structure over the well at the exact apex of the moon's orbit called the lunar standstill, which occurs every 18.6 years.

Another astronomical alignment in the region is built on the island nation of Malta, only 400 miles away from Sardinia. On the south coast of the main island of Malta is a temple called Mnajdra. It's laid out in a trefoil pattern made up of three circles. One of the three temples is a solar calendar tracking the equinoxes. Another one of them tracks the solstices.

Mainstream archaeologists say these structures were built between 4,500 and 5,600 years ago, but the astrological alignments point to a much, much more ancient period. For example, University of Malta Professor Paul Micallef discovered an astronomical alignment at Mnajdra that dates the temple to a much earlier time. He published a book, "Mnajdra Prehistoric Temple: A Calendar in Stone," claiming that 12,200 years ago, precisely at sunrise on the summer solstice, a sun beam would shine down the main corridor of the temple and hit the center of the main altar stone. Due to the precession, the position of the sun beam has changed, but Micallef was able to extrapolate the number of years ago, the beam would have shone on the altar. [140] [141] [142]

We believe it is likely that mainstream archaeology is dating many of these ancient sites incorrectly. Stone cannot be dated. The way archaeologists date stone structures is to perform carbon dating on the detritus found around them. But, we believe this will always lead to incorrect conclusions. When the sites were in use by the people who built them, they would have kept them clean, detritus would not be permitted to accumulate; and would not be there until after the sites had been abandoned. It is also possible the sites were abandoned by their original builders, and then discovered by another later culture, who removed the detritus and then repurposed the sites for their own use and later abandoned them again. Only the detritus of the second culture would be there. The construction then became attributed to this later culture, which did not have the technological skills necessary to build them, as in the case with the Inca.

This brings us to the fascinating work of Mark Carlotto, Ph.D., an engineer, scientist and author with almost forty years of experience in satellite imaging, remote sensing, image processing and pattern recognition. He has written seven books and has proposed a theory that many of the ancient megalithic sites around the world are much older than previously believed.

Ancient monument builders almost always built their structures in some kind of cosmic alignment, usually on the cardinal points. [143]

While studying the ancient sites of Mesoamerica, especially Teotihuacan, Carlotto was puzzled by how the pyramids did not align with the cardinal points; he couldn't understand this discrepancy until he took the crustal displacement theories of Hapgood into account. When he calculated the alignment of the Pyramid of the Sun at Teotihuacan and other sites in the region, he found that their alignments were consistent with each other, but off the cardinal points by several degrees. But, when he extrapolated the points to the previous position of the North Pole on the east Hudson Bay, they aligned perfectly. Hapgood surmised the Hudson Bay pole existed between 18,000 to 12,000 years ago. Carlotto discovered that if the original site of Teotihuacan, and all the other sites in the area, were laid out to align with the cardinal points, then they must have been established at least 12,000 years ago.

As hard as this calculation is to take in and believe, it's nothing to the conclusions Carlotto drew from the Temple of Jupiter, Temple Mount in Jerusalem and the Acropolis of ancient Greece. The original sites of these structures align to the pole when it was in Greenland, roughly 50,000 years ago.

The oldest site discovered by Carlotto's method was the Temple of the Sun at Ollantaytambo in Peru. One would presume a "sun" temple would align to the cardinal points. But, when Carlotto extrapolated the alignment of this site, he found it lined up with the pole when it was located in the Bering Sea, 100,000 years ago.

Carlotto believes that many of these sites could have been destroyed and rebuilt on the older original sites on top of the ruins of older structures that aligned to the older poles. He put forth the possibility that a previous technological civilization could have developed from an early migration of modern humans from Africa. Which would also explain the African features on the stone heads of the Olmecs.

If Carlotto's theory is correct, we must attribute all these sites to people living many thousands of years before recorded history. Before the devastation of the Hiawatha impact erased all traces of them except for their colossal stone monuments, the only thing that can stand the test of time.

CHAPTER TWELVE

INEXPLICABLE ANCIENT SUMERIAN KNOWLEDGE

Another unexplained mystery of the ancient world is the fully developed ancient Sumerian civilization. Archaeologists believe this society began nearly 6,000 years ago and is considered to be one of the earliest civilizations on the planet, but in spite of being one of the oldest, it was incredibly advanced. It seems to have been created out of nowhere with no precursor or traceable evolution.

Ancient Mesopotamian cultures were located in what is now modern day Iraq, between the Tigris and Euphrates Rivers, an area that is now referred to as the Fertile Crescent.

In 1849, British archaeologist Austen Layard discovered 30,000 clay tablets in the ancient city of Nineveh, in northern Iraq: the Royal Library of Ashurbanipal. [137] [144]

In the 20th century several scholars set about translating the tablets.

At this point we must introduce the researcher, scholar and author Zecharia Sitchin and his theories about the Anunnaki, the gods of ancient Mesopotamia. Sitchin was one of the few scholars able to translate ancient Sumerian, Akkadian and Babylonian cuneiform writing. He wrote twelve books on the subject of these ancient societies and the history of their gods.

These ancient texts, conveniently written on clay tablets and fired so as to be readable 6,000 years later, were not written like mythological stories, but in dry factual accounts as if they were actual events. A lot of the tablets contained inventories, accounting information and everyday record keeping, but mixed in these mundane archives were accounts of the Anunnaki.

The primary players of the Sumerian pantheon are Anu, two of his sons, Enlil and Ea, his daughter, Sud, Enlil's son and heir, Ninurta, Ea's son and heir, Marduk, and Enlil's granddaughter, Inanna, who were among the council of the twelve ruling Anunnaki.

In his first book, *The 12th Planet*, Sitchin writes about the inexplicable accomplishments of the ancient Sumerians. [137]

The Sumerian civilization, located in the southernmost part of the region, was the earliest of all the ancient Mesopotamian cultures but it was not the first to be discovered. Excavations began in the northern part of the area, in the cities of the Babylonian civilization. The writings pointed to the Akkadian civilization as preceding the Babylonian. Then it was discovered that Akkadian writings were again a derived language from even older writings. Eventually the earliest discovered civilization in the area was in Sumer.

The Sumerian civilization was so advanced, they were assumed to be a derivative one as well, but no evidence of a prior civilization in the region was to be discovered. As far as anyone could tell, the Sumerians were the first, established in about 3,800 B.C., nearly 6,000 years ago.

Sumerians were responsible for many of mankind's "firsts," frequently attributed to much later civilizations.

They were highly advanced astronomers who knew about the existence of all the outer planets of our solar system, even Pluto. How did they know about all the outer planets? Good question. Sumerian astronomy was unparalleled until we reached the twentieth century. It is completely unexplainable without attributing it to an advanced unknown derivative civilization. They even had an extraordinary calendar.

The Sumerians were also very interested in astrology and they created an early version of the zodiac. Their version called Taurus "the heavenly bull," Cancer "the pincers or tongs," Libra "the heavenly fate," Scorpio "that which claws and cuts," Capricorn the "goat fish," and Aquarius "lord of the waters." Aries the ram is "field dweller" and Virgo, called AB.SIN, meaning the daughter of the Sumerian/Akkadian god Nannar/Sin, is the virgin. The other designations essentially remain unchanged; Gemini is "twins," Leo is "lion," Pisces is "the fishes" and Sagittarius "the archer."

The Sumerians had a complete written language with a complex alphabet, lexicon and dictionary, with the first known methods of printing. They used clay cylinders rolled onto clay tablets and pictograph type used like rubber stamps.

They describe agriculture, irrigation and granaries with grain measurements. Early writings describe gardens and brick-lined wells. We find descriptions of the first domesticated animals. They had a textile industry with woven cloth.

They had methods of firing bricks in kilns and other clay products, the first cities with complex architecture describing the building of temples, watch towers, fortresses, houses and enormous ziggurats, built with reinforced concrete. Sumerian cities were built with sewer systems and archaeologists discovered pavements with limestone pavers as old as the fourth millennium B.C.

They described the construction of docks for ships. They had trading networks shipping grains and ores from mining operations. Silver was being mined in the Taurus Mountains at the north end of Mesopotamia, gold was being shipped from Africa, cedars from Lebanon and hardwoods from Ararat. Metals were cast into tools, utensils and ornaments, all being produced in the third millennium B.C.

A monetary system was in place, with prices set for grain measurements and other trade items.

The Sumerian system of mathematics was a sexagesimal one, with a base figure of sixty, which is very easy to break into fractions, made for the easy calculating of roots and multiplying in powers. Our method of dividing a circle into 360 degrees originated in the Sumerian culture.

The Sumerians had a legal system with courts, contracts and judges.

They had jobs, wages and taxes. Scribes were a common job in ancient Sumeria, these people were the record keepers for the society.

The ancient Sumerians had paints, glazes, extensive plant-based and mineral-based medicines, prescriptions, doctors, midwives and veterinarians and were even performing surgeries. They had clay models of human organs and an extensive knowledge of human anatomy.

They produced alcohol both for disinfection and consumption, they brewed beer, made wine and collected honey.

Agriculture was extensive. They milled grains into flour for breads, pastries and biscuits. They grew fruit orchards.

They processed meats including pork, mutton and poultry. They had a farmer's almanac. They consumed dairy products produced from sheep's, cow's and goat's milk.

Cooking was an art form with written recipes.

They had efficient methods of transportation, with roads and ships. They used the wheel on carts and chariots and described ox power and horsepower.

They were accomplished in the arts, in poetry, theater, jewelry, music and song. Their music used the heptatonic scale.

There were schools and classes, curriculums, teachers and historians.

They had a bicameral congress system of laws and punishments long before Hammurabi, who got his ideas from a Sumerian king of Ur called Urnammu in 2350 B.C., who started the concepts of justice and righteousness.

Even some evil "firsts" can be attributed to the Sumerians. They had the first known records of political corruption, fraud and thievery.

The list of societal firsts goes on and on.

How can all these accomplishments have come out of nowhere? The answer is, they can't have. This is another impossible thing. Unless we take the Sumerians at their word and believe them when they wrote that they had learned everything they knew from the Anunnaki, their gods, who created them, taught them, cared for them, punished them, controlled them and used them as their labor force. When they were the teachers of the ancient Sumerians, the Anunnaki were the origin of nearly all the civilizations of the Earth. [137]

CHAPTER THIRTEEN

THE BABYLONIAN CREATION MYTH

A fascinating story from ancient Babylonia is the Enuma Elish creation story. An ancient Sumerian creation story, the precursor to the Babylonian one, was said to exist, but so far has been lost to modern-day scholars.

So the Babylonian version must suffice for now.

The story describes the formation of our solar system, told thousands of years ago, and includes the existence of Pluto, Neptune and all the distant outer planets we'd only finished discovering in the twentieth century. As mentioned above, the ancient Sumerians somehow knew about these planets six thousand years ago.

Sitchin translated the story and related the full version in his first book, but the reader will find a summarized version here.

One of the most interesting things about this story is it offers an explanation of the formation of our solar system. There are several unexplained mysteries about our system that find plausible explanations in this ancient story. It explains the creation of the Earth and our inexplicably large moon. It also describes how the asteroid belt was created. Scientists have long been puzzled as to why Earth has such a huge moon, much bigger in ratio to any other planet and satellite in our system. The formation of the asteroid belt has also been a mystery. Studies of asteroids that have fallen to Earth show that these celestial bodies are composed of minerals that are only formed inside the cores of planets. The belt used to be a planet. What happened to it? How did a planet become a debris field?

The most recent theory attempting to explain the formation of our large moon, the giant impact theory, proposes that in the early development of our solar system another forming planet crashed into the earth and the two bodies reformed into our planet and our moon. But, according to planetary science researcher Professor Sara Russell, of the Natural History Museum, this theory has a problem: moon rocks are proving that the Earth and the moon have "some remarkable chemical and isotopic similarities; suggesting they have a linked history." In other words, the Earth and the moon are made of the same materials in the same proportions. [145]

The Babylonian creation myth explains not only the creation and positioning of our planet and moon, it also explains why the moon is made of the same stuff as Earth. It also explains the asteroid belt, created by the destruction of a planet that used to exist between Mars and Jupiter.

The Enuma Elish describes the entrance of the twelfth planet, Nibiru, into our solar system. The ruler of ancient Babylonia was Marduk, so in the Babylonian version of the creation story, Marduk is the hero planet, and all references to Nibiru are replaced with Marduk. It is presumed that the lost Sumerian version would have had Anu as the hero, replacing the name of Nibiru with Anu.

In this story, the planets are named as the ancient gods of Sumeria, but Sitchin was able to surmise which planet is which.

The story begins with the formation of the sun. Then one by one and in order of all the most inner planets, Mercury, Venus and Mars came into being. After Mars comes Tiamat, described as a large water world. Then came the formation of Jupiter and Saturn, with Pluto next to Saturn as his son, then a pair of twin planets comparable in size to Saturn – obviously Uranus and Neptune. Neptune is named after Marduk's father, Ea, also called Enki.

The next phase of the story tells of the great cosmic collisions. Created in the deep of space, coming from outside the solar system, is the planet Marduk (Nibiru), the son of Ea, who bore him by drawing him into the solar system. From this, we surmise that the gravity of Neptune pulled Nibiru into our solar system as it was doing a flyby.

Marduk was still molten and not fully formed, and was very large. Marduk's moons were called "winds" in the story. As Marduk passed by Uranus, four of his "winds" were pulled from his side, becoming satellites of Uranus.

Marduk continues to fall through our solar system until he passes by Tiamat, disturbing her orbit. Tiamat begins growing and starts producing "monsters" (satellites of her own). The first born of her monsters is called Kingu, Tiamat's hero and protector.

Tiamat begins raging and becomes unstable, "scaring" the other planets or gods, who fear her and cannot tame her. We infer from this that the passage of Nibiru so close to Tiamat made the planet's orbit so unstable as to threaten the existence of other planets in the solar system.

Saturn names Marduk as the hero who will slay Kingu and do battle with Tiamat.

As Marduk passes Saturn, he throws Pluto from his course as a messenger to the outer gods. The gods are grateful for Marduk's willingness to fight Tiamat and the gods name Marduk as their king.

So, now Marduk's orbit is set on a collision course with Tiamat. To prepare for battle, Marduk brings forth three more winds, and two of these satellites collide with Tiamat, tearing her in half, slaying her. Her host of satellites are set running in fear to become comets that are dragged out of the inner system by Marduk's net (gravity) and into their strange orbits.

All Tiamat's satellites are lost except Kingu.

On Marduk's next orbit through our solar system, he again approached the killed Tiamat and Kingu. Kingu had temporarily become a planet in his own right because his orbit was changed by Marduk's first pass, and though he was still near Tiamat, he was orbiting the sun.

During his second orbit through our solar system, Marduk himself struck Tiamat, separating her head from her body and blending the waters of the two planets together; transferring the seeds of life from Marduk to Tiamat. After he struck her, another of Marduk's satellites struck her head, and the heavy blow moved her head into a new orbit where no planet had been orbiting before, (this was now Earth), and Kingu followed behind her head, and started orbiting her again, becoming our moon.

The body of Tiamat was smashed in the collision with Marduk, becoming the asteroid belt.

Marduk's huge orbit through our solar system of 3,600 years was now established.

The planets were then in the orbits we know today. Pluto was dragged into its bizarre, elliptical-and-tilted outer orbit, a large portion of Tiamat was broken off to become our Earth and a satellite made of her body became our moon, which is why it is composed of the same minerals as the Earth.

The rest of Tiamat was smashed into the rubble that now makes up the asteroid belt. Our solar system's comets were satellites of Tiamat that were dragged out of the inner system into their wild Oort-Cloud-visiting, elliptical orbits.

And Nibiru is a visitor to our solar system that passes through between Mars and Jupiter every 3,600 years.

This fantastic story would be completely unbelievable, except that it happens to fit the facts of the order and existence of the satellites in our solar system.

We've already said that the ancient Sumerians knew of the existence of all the outer planets including Pluto. The Sumerians count the planets of our solar system as twelve, and we find it of particular interest that they count them from the outside inward. Pluto is number one, Neptune is two, Uranus is three, Saturn is four, Jupiter is five, Mars is six, Earth is seven, Earth's moon which at one point had a solar orbit is eight, Venus is nine, Mercury is ten and the sun is eleven. Marduk, or Nibiru, is the twelfth planet, hence the title of Sitchin's first book. [137]

CHAPTER FOURTEEN

FOLLOW THE SUPPRESSION

Are aliens involved at all, and what do the ancient Sumerians have to do with current UFO activity?

Why are all these alien races so similar to humans?

In fact the Nordics are almost indistinguishable from humans. They are described as tall (between six and seven feet), blond, blue-eyed, fair-skinned, beautiful, benevolent, telepathic, paternal, affectionate, youthful, caring, concerned about the environment, with Aryan features and slightly Germanic accents. [146]

Less human looking, but still humanoids are the Greys. Rare photos of Grey aliens leaked to the media over the years show them as having nipples, proving they evolved from lactating mammals.

Even the descriptions of the Reptilian aliens are not drastically different from humans. They are still described as humanoids, but with scaly skin.

If all these creatures are truly aliens from other worlds, then why are they so similar to humans?

In our opinion, a lot of clues to the truth can be found in government suppression. If you are trying to keep something secret, you have to suppress the evidence. Suppression can come in a variety of forms. You can steal the evidence, hide it away and then lie about its existence, you can discredit the evidence to make everyone believe it's not real, you can ignore the evidence and hope it fades away by itself or you can destroy the evidence and make the destruction look like something other than suppression.

In searching for the truth, we have been laser focused on suppression when we find it. Let's examine a few examples of suppression.

Giants once existed. If you don't know this, then you are a victim of suppression. Most of the time when giant skeletons have been discovered, they disappear. Someone spirits away the evidence and it is never seen again. Why aren't these discoveries common knowledge? In a word: suppression. [147]

What we are talking about here are people who are naturally of gigantic stature, living healthy lives with average lifespans, as opposed to persons suffering from acromegaly gigantism, a pituitary gland condition that leaves visible traces on the skeletal remains such as hypercalcification and excessive, exaggerated bone growth and causes shortened lifespans.

Richard J. Dewhurst, the author of *The Ancient Giants Who Ruled America: The Missing Skeletons and the Great Smithsonian Cover-Up,* said of the Smithsonian Institute's suppression of all information regarding the discoveries of giant human skeletal remains, "What my research has revealed is that the Smithsonian has been at the center of a vast cover-up of America's true history since the 1880s." [148]

And, "After the Civil War the Smithsonian began to adopt a policy of excluding any evidence of direct foreign influence in the Americas prior to Columbus."

Dewhurst was convinced the Smithsonian had adopted a policy of altering evidence to suit their theories of European introduction to the Americas and put on blinders to any evidence that differed from their view of history. This is once again a perversion of mainstream academia's role of finding the truth whether it jibes with your preconceived notions or not. Obviously, an ancient North American occupation of red-haired giants seven thousands years ago would be counter to their belief that Christopher Columbus was the first European to ever set foot on North American soil.

Jason Colavito has compiled a very large list of newspaper articles about the discovery of gigantic skeletal remains in North America that can easily be viewed online. There are over one hundred of these articles posted on the site. [149]

We've cited some examples below, mostly leaving out incidents of a single skeleton find or any articles with incomplete information.

An article "Remains of Giants Found in Arkansas: Human Skeletons Unearthed Eight and Ten Feet in Height" was printed in the *Memphis Daily Appeal,* on August 28, 1870.

An Indian mound two miles west of Barfield Park, Arkansas, was called the Chicasawba, derived from the name of a Shawnee chief. When an excavation was made near the foot of the mound, a portion of a gigantic human skeleton was found. The skull easily fit over the head of the reporting party. The huge human would have stood between eight and nine feet tall. A long-necked earthen jar was found under the head.

Further excavating uncovered similar skeletons with similar vases.

"It is not a matter of doubt that these are HUMAN REMAINS, but of a long extinct race — a race which flourished, lived, and died many centuries ago, in those days told of in Scripture. ('And there were Giants in those days.')"

An article, "Niagara's Ancient Cemetery of Giants," printed in the *Daily Telegraph,* of Toronto, Ontario, Canada, on August 23, 1871, described an ancient settlement of giants found with axes, skimmers and stone pipes. Two hundred skeletons, each wearing necklaces of stone beads, were discovered on a farm belonging to the Reverend Nathaniel Wardell in a township known as Cayuga. The largest of the skeletons were nine feet tall and only a few were under seven feet. The thigh bones were "at least a foot longer than those at present known, and one of the skulls being examined completely covered the head of an ordinary person."

The ground at this farm had been cultivated for over a century and was covered by a pine forest before that time.

An article, "A Cave of Dead Indian Mammoth Remains," was reluctantly printed in the *Daily State Journal,* of Richmond, Virginia, on September 6, 1871, describing a catacomb of giant skeletons found with stone arrows and mortars. The paper was reluctant because of the fantastic subject matter, but went ahead because they trusted their reliable source who'd handled the evidence himself.

Railroad workers found the catacomb between Weldon and Garysburg, North Carolina, "The femur being as long as the leg of an ordinary man, the stature of the body being probably as great as eight or nine feet."

An article, "The Early American Giant," in the *New York Times*, printed on February 8, 1876, described the discovery of three giant skeletons in Kentucky.

Two men exploring a cave near Louisville found a vault with three skeletons of individuals of about nine feet tall.

An article, "Remains of Nine-Foot Giants in Ohio," in the *Marion Daily Star,* printed on July 14, 1880, described a particularly important find.

Two giant skeletons were discovered in a grave in a mound in Muskingum County, Ohio; one was a nine-foot, four-inch tall male and an eight-foot-tall female.

In another grave a woman's skeleton was found in a clay coffin. She had a three-and-a half-foot-long child in her arms. Seven more skeletons were found in the mound; the smallest was nine feet in height and the largest was ten feet.

A stone resting against the clay coffin bore two lines of strange hieroglyphs.

An article, "Giant Crowned Royalty is Found," published in the *Ban-*

ner, of Athens, Georgia, on May 6, 1884, is one of the earliest accounts of all the evidence being sent to the Smithsonian, which has now disappeared. This find was called "the most interesting collection ever found in America."

An Indian mound in Cartersville, Georgia, was investigated by a committee of scientists sent from the Smithsonian. Under a layer of hand-carved, dressed flagstones a vault was found that contained a giant mummy measuring seven feet, two inches. The stones exhibited carved hieroglyphs.

The mummy had waist-length black hair and a copper crown. Near the mummy were the bodies of several children of varying sizes covered in beads. The bodies had been "prepared somewhat after the manner of mummies."

The Smithsonian personnel then began excavating similar mounds in the area.

An article, "Skeletons Seven Feet Long," was published in the *New York Times,* on May 5, 1885, detailing a find of giant skeletons in Centerburg, Ohio.

School boys opened a small mound and found a large vault housing four giant skeletons. Three were over seven feet in length and the fourth was over eight feet. They were found with thirty stone implements and vessels and a "curiously-wrought pipe."

Sometimes the number of skeletons found is very large, indicating a settlement as opposed to wandering visitors. An article, "Giants Found on the New York-Pennsylvania State Line," printed in the *Philadelphia Times,* on June 27, 1885, describes the find of 150 giant skeletons.

Workmen on the farm of J.H. Porter found the entrance to a cave where heaps of giant human bones were piled. Many of the skeletons were complete and measured by scientists who said, "They are the remains of a race of gigantic creatures, compared with which our tallest men would appear pygmies. There are no arrow-heads, stone hatchets, or other implements of war with the bodies. Some of the bones are on exhibition at the various stores."

An article, "A Race of Indian Giants," that ran in the *New York Times,* on February 9, 1890, described a find in Pleasantville, New Jersey. Crowds flocked to the site of an "Indian graveyard." The first "lot" was eight bodies "closely laid together in a deep chamber, snugly packed in with tortoise, oyster, and clam shells."

"The owners of the land, gave to the Archaeological Association of the University of Pennsylvania the right to search for relics on their land."

Weapons and ornamental decorations were found with the bodies.

A total of fifty bodies were exhumed; some were children, some were seven feet and one, presumed to be an old medicine man, was eight feet.

Here we've made an exception to our single-skeleton rule because it has an accompanying photo. This famous picture accompanied a discovery of a large human mummy in San Diego, California, published in *The World,* on October 7, 1895.

The mummy measured over eight feet long, but was estimated to be nine feet tall in life. The mummy was inspected by a curator of the Smithsonian Institute.

Prospectors discovered the mummy in a cave.

Sometimes members of this race of gigantic individuals were found to have "double rows of teeth." An article, "The Vanished Race: A Building That Housed 6,000 Cliff Dwellers," printed in the *Washington Bee,* on November 4, 1899, was one such find.

The find describes a "ruined aboriginal city" high on a cliff in southeastern Colorado and New Mexico. Some "remarkable relics" were also described.

An excavation of a cliff over the Santa Fe River near Espanola, New Mexico, yielded stone implements, pottery, skulls with two rows of teeth

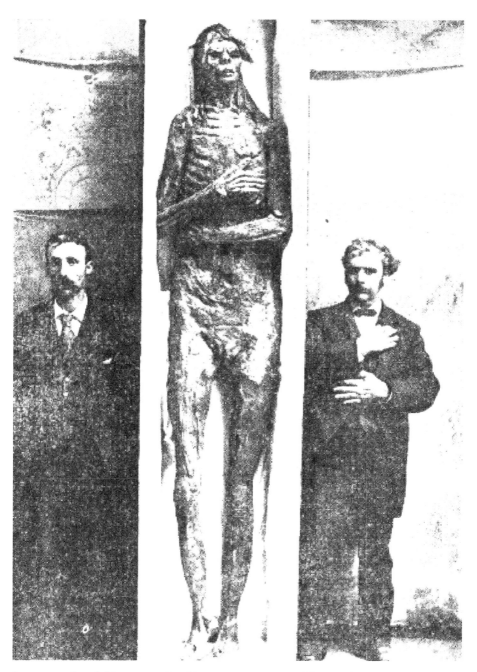

Prospectors found this mummy in 1895 near San Diego, California. The mummy was examined by Professor Thomas Wilson, curator of the Department of Prehistoric Anthropology at the Smithsonian Institute. The professor thought the individual would have been nine feet tall in life.

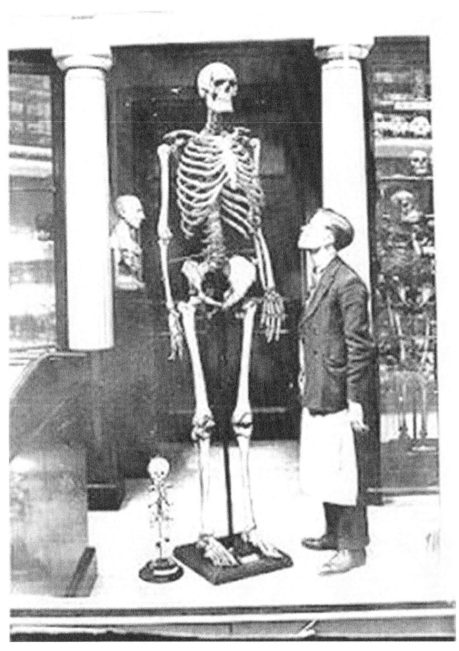

The giant skeleton in this old newspaper photo was supposed to have come from a West Virginia burial mound excavated in the 1800s. Photo credit unknown.

"and the bones of a race all of whose teeth were molars or grinders. Among the bones excavated from a burial mound on the mesa were a woman's femurs measuring nineteen inches, a length which indicates that this aboriginal giantess must have been at least seven and a half feet tall."

Communal cliff dweller buildings were discovered here, "of nobody knows how many centuries ago." The settlement was estimated to have a "population averaged about three to a room, which would make between 4,800 and six thousand people dwelling in the immense pueblo, besides those who lived in the cliff caves."

Another find described these unusual dental anomalies. An article, "Double-Toothed Giant," published in the *Journal Tribune*, of Williamsburg, Iowa, on April 27, 1900, describes the discovery made in Hardin County, now called the Booda Collection.

A skeleton found in a mound on the banks of the Iowa River near Eagle City was said to be very large and, "A set of almost round double teeth are remarkably well preserved. They are yellow with age, are perfect in shape, and appear to have been double, both above and below. The femurs are very long, showing a giant in stature."

A rare collection of implements were also found. The skeleton was examined by a physician who said it was "that of a person who had evidently been trained for athletics, as the extremities were so well developed."

An article, "Giants' Skeletons Found: Cave in Mexico Gives Up the Bones of an Ancient Race," was published in the *New York TImes*, on May 4, 1908.

Charles C. Clapp, who was in charge of a mine in Mexico, discovered two hundred skeletons of men, "each above eight feet in height. The cave was evidently the burial place of a race of giants who antedated the Aztecs."

An article, "Skeletons Discovered in Wisconsin are Larger Than Present Men," was published in the *New York Times*, on May 4, 1912.

The article stated that the many skeletons discovered at Lake Delavan and Lake Lawn Farm were declared to be an "unknown race of men [who] inhabited Southern Wisconsin ages ago."

The heads were found to be "much larger than those of any people which inhabit America today."

An article, "Report of Sixty-Eight Skeletons Averaging Seven-Feet Tall," was published by the *Charleston Daily Mail,* on September 20, 1916. The excavation of a mound at Tioga Point, near Sayre, Pennsylvania, uncovered sixty-eight skeletons. The average height was seven feet with many of them even taller. They were found with huge axes.

The Charleston find was also described on another website.

The "Legends of America" website has information about these discoveries and a collection of photos taken of these huge skeletons. On the page are dozens of discoveries from the 1700s through to the early 1920s. According to this site, the skeletons ranged in height from six feet seven inches to ten feet nine inches tall, with teeth the size of horse teeth. Many of them displayed elongated skulls. The giants are frequently buried with normal humans, but the giants figured prominently in the burial sites, buried in central locations with other skeletons surrounding them, or on "thrones" with "stone tools and flint artifacts." [147]

Word of these discoveries drew the attention of the Smithsonian Institute , which sent a team of scientists to West Virginia in 1883 to study the phenomenon.

At the "Legends of America" site, this is described: "[T]he Smithsonian Institute dispatched a team of archaeologists to the Criel Mound in South Charleston. Led by Colonel Lewis Morris, the team conducted extensive digs of some fifty mounds in the area and issued a detailed report."

Where is this "detailed report?" Good question.

"In their investigation, the team uncovered numerous giants, one of which was seven foot six inches tall and decorated with six heavy copper bracelets on each wrist, and on his shoulder were three large plates of mica. In another mound, they found a circle of ten normal human skeletons surrounding one giant skeleton in the middle, as well as underground vaults, various copper and mica ornaments, jewelry, religious items, pipes and spearheads. Another large skeleton was also found that had a 'flat-head' type skull." [147]

More giant skeletons were found by dean of American archaeology Warren Moorehead on August 19, 1922, on a beach in Milford, Connecticut. His excavations uncovered the remains of two massive giants; their discovery sparked a media sensation at the time, but since then, evidence of the discovery has been suppressed. [150]

There is a story told by the Paiute tribe, local to Utah and Nevada in the US, of a battle fought with white, red-haired giants. The Paiutes and other tribes wanted to get rid of these vicious people and the story tells how they cornered them in a cave and set fire to the entrance. The story gained credibility when in 1926, a mining company discovered mummified remains in Lovelock Caves in Nevada. They reported the find of artifacts and two red-haired giants, a man over eight feet tall and a woman six-and-a-half feet tall to archaeologists. Two more eight-foot-tall skeletons were discovered near the area of the caves in 1931. [151]

"Legends of America" also references the *New York Times*, article on the Wisconsin finds of 1912.

The *New York Times* reported a find on May 4, 1912, at Delavan Lake, Wisconsin. Two boys found eighteen skeletons between seven and nine feet tall. They were submitted to the State Historical Museum and later confiscated by the Smithsonian Museum. [152]

Another documented report of giants was when in 1892 scientists from the University of Montpellier in France studied bones that had been excavated on France's Mediterranean coast and found that they belonged to a human who stood over eleven feet tall. Where are these remains today? No additional references can be found.

The same suppression of giant skeletons happened on the islands of Malta and Sardinia.

These discoveries have also been suppressed. The skeletons were frequently reported as "stolen" or "disappeared" in some other way, and are no longer available for modern day DNA testing. [141]

The ancient Nuraghe were building giant tombs on the island of Sardinia, Italy, in the distant past; around eight hundred of them have been found. Some believe they were building these megalithic structures about six thousand years ago, while others believe they were building them 12,000 years ago. When these tombs were excavated, huge skeletons were sometimes discovered in them.

In the town of Porto Torres, Sardinia, in 1953, excavators uncovered two eight-foot-tall skeletons, found with grave implements and weapons. These remains are missing.

Another example of this suppression took place with the excavations in the town of Sardara. Multiple nine-foot-tall skeletons were found under the church of Sant' Anastasia. They were placed inside the church and disappeared overnight. [141]

In the late 1920s a Peruvian archaeologist named Julio Tello found hundreds of cone-shaped skulls in the Paracas region of Peru. These skulls were missing the sagittal suture that is found on all normal human skulls. This find could not be covered up so easily and many of the skulls are still in museums and private collections. But suppression has been happening in the form of discrediting. Some of these skulls have had DNA testing, and the testing is showing them to be human, a fact widely touted to the media as proof these skulls are not aliens'. But, only mitochondrial DNA (DNA from the mother) was extracted, proving the mother to be a human. No information about the father could be extracted. One DNA test on one of these skulls showed mitochondrial human DNA from the area of Scotland. The question now becomes, what is Scottish DNA doing in ancient misshapen Peruvian skulls? We now need to consider whether Tuatha De Danann's influence ever extended into the New World. [55] [153]

There is another astounding piece of early architecture that is also associated with giants. On the island nation of Malta is found the Hal Saflieni Hypogeum. An ancient underground structure of amazing complexity, it was built with huge stones with no mortar, requiring an advanced level of engineering principles. It was built in antiquity by nobody knows who.

Discovered there were skeletons with elongated, giant skulls that displayed many strange abnormalities and also had no sagittal sutures. When the skeletons were discovered, there were thousands of them reported, but the later reports said only one hundred had been found.

This story was suppressed.

The first official excavator of the site, Emmanuel Magri, never got his find published and all his notebooks on the excavation disappeared after his death in 1907.

The Hypogeum has since been closed off with no more excavations allowed. [154] [155] [156]

Suppression, suppression, suppression!

Many years ago I read a story about a woman's strange experience deep in the caverns under the Hypogeum before they were eventually closed off to visitors. I haven't been able to find the book and I don't remember its title, but I found an account of the story online. [157]

A woman and some of her friends went on a tour of the caves with a local. She asked her guide what was through another cave they came to. She was told she would need a rope to descend down through it. The cave was small; she and one of her friends had to crouch down to get through. They were using flame torches. At the end of the cave she came to a short ledge over a long drop in a very large cavern.

While she was standing on the ledge, she saw a cave on the other side and below with a group of nine-foot-tall human-like creatures coming out of it in single file. They turned to her and beckoned her to come down to them. She became very frightened, especially when her torch blew out.

Her friend was behind her, and hadn't seen the men. They managed to backtrack and rejoin their party.

The online article also includes a story about a missing group of children and their teacher who were lost in the Hypogeum, never to be found.

I include this strange story even though it is the account of a single person because it tells yet another tale about giant, human-like beings who reside deep inside our planet.

Even when not fully suppressed, finds of giant skeletons almost never reach mainstream news.

A research team led by British anthropologist Russell Dement claims half a dozen human skeletons, between seven and eight feet tall, have recently been discovered in the Amazon region of Ecuador. Dement heard about the discovery in late 2013, and went to investigate. The skeletons are presently undergoing examination in Germany.

We'll have to wait and see to find out if this discovery will be suppressed, but it sure didn't make the evening news, did it? [158]

Why? Why are these discoveries so important and the knowledge so volatile that it must be hidden? And, all the suppression can't be attributed to the Smithsonian Institute alone because it is taking place in Europe too.

Another bizarre and deeply disturbing wave of suppression involves the antiquities of ancient Iraq, Syria and Libya. Since 2014, ancient Sumerian, Babylonian, Akkadian and Assyrian art and texts have been destroyed in a strange attempted ethnocide. The perpetrators are ostensibly claiming to be religious zealots purging the idolatrous heretical doctrines of the past.

But what is strange, is these perps are reportedly very organized operatives, dressed like government officials with earpieces in their ears. [159] [160]

Who is really behind this destruction of the ancient evidence of the origins of human civilization?

By following the suppression, we gain clues as to who might be covering up evidence and who might be hiding their existence from us.

The answer to the mysteries of the giants may lie in antiquity. In the Old Testament, at the part when God resolved to destroy mankind by flooding the world, it talks about the sons of the deities, the Nephilim, or giants, who married the daughters of men who were upon the Earth. That's "deities" plural.

The Old Testament book of Enoch, who was Noah's great-grandfather, was removed from the Bible in the fourth century A.D. by the Council of Laodicea. Many scholars believe the removal was due to the passage in his writing that talks about rebellious angels who were in trouble with God for mating with humans. The passage says, "200 angels disobey God came to earth and mated with human women."

There are references in ancient Kabbalistic teachings about Adam himself being a giant and that the Adamic race, the first modern humans, being of a gigantic stature. Much larger than the human beings of today. [161]

CHAPTER FIFTEEN

WHAT DO ANCIENT SUMERIAN GODS HAVE TO DO WITH ALIENS?

Another civilization who described ancient giants in their past were the Sumerians. The ancient Sumerian gods, the Anunnaki, were said to be of gigantic stature, and it is the Anunnaki who actually claim to be the creators of modern man.

It's a bit daunting to try to relate the conclusions of a genius like Sitchin in a few chapters. He laid out his many theories in his twelve books, the first seven of which were called the "Earth Chronicles" series. Essentially Sitchin proposed that we take ancient stories of Sumer as literal, historical fact.

In his books, Sitchin makes a very convincing case, proving many connections of ancient Sumerian, Akkadian and Babylonian stories to other theogenies, like the myths of ancient Greece, the Old Testament, the Vedic Texts of India, the accounts of the early Egyptian pantheon and many other kingdoms and cultures.

The word "Anunnaki" means "those who from heaven to earth came," and the "Nephilim," "those who were cast down." Sitchin gives a meticulous explanation of who the Anunnaki were, when they came here, what they were after and what they did on our planet. [137]

Sitchin's translations of Sumerian tablets tell how the Anunnaki came from a planet called Nibiru, which circles a brown dwarf star in our vicinity and has a huge, 3,600-year elliptical orbit. At the apogee of this orbit, Nibiru passes through our solar system in the gap between Mars and Jupiter.

The possible existence of a nearby brown dwarf was discovered in 1983 by the Infrared Astronomical Satellite (IRAS), a space-based orbiting telescope funded by the US, the Netherlands and the UK.

The discovered "heavenly body" is close enough to Earth (fifty billion miles away) that it may be part of our solar system. This sounds like a huge distance, but is relatively close by cosmological measurements.

The object is the size of Jupiter and it is in the direction of the constellation Orion.

A *Washington Post* article, "Orbiting eye reveals mystery space monster" (December 30, 1983) described the discovery. At the time Dr. Gerry Neugebauer, IRAS chief scientist for California's Jet Propulsion Laboratory and director of the Palomar Observatory for the California Institute of Technology, was not sure what the object was, speculating that, among other possibilities, it might be a "protostar that never became hot enough to become a star," also known as a brown dwarf. Brown dwarf stars do exist, but they are so dark, they can only be spotted by infrared telescopes. [162]

Some of the other possibilities were that the object might be a planet or a giant comet, but these were discounted when it was discovered that the object did not change its position over a six month period of time.

This article can no longer be found in the *Washington Post*, archive, but it can be seen on the Rabbit Hole website. [163]

When it came out, the article caused a cacophony of debate about the existence of Nibiru. Articles named it Plant X, Nemesis and The Destroyer Planet of Hercolubus. Several articles about our solar system having a dark star companion and possibly being a binary system with a brown dwarf surfaced.

Uranus and Neptune orbital perturbations have been discovered and were described in a *Newsweek*, article, "Does the Sun Have a Dark Companion?," published on June 28, 1982, which now cannot be found in its original form on the internet.

A portion of this article is also online at the Rabbit Hole website. In it, John Anderson of JPL commented on the strange anomalies of Uranus and Neptune: "[T]his odd behavior suggests that the sun has an unseen companion, a dark star gravitationally bound to it but billions of miles away." [164]

These and other articles confirming the possible existence of Nibiru have mysteriously been scrubbed from the internet. In our opinion, this is possible evidence of more suppression.

Other thin, but interesting evidence for the possible existence of Nibiru can be found in the work of researcher Hugh Harleston (mentioned in Chapter 10), who surmised the layout of the structures along the Avenue of the Dead at Teotihuacan was a map of our solar system.

Harleston discovered a distant temple along the exact eye line of the Avenue of the Dead. If this temple represents another planet in our solar system, then it is twice as far away as Pluto. [165]

Sumerian texts definitely report the existence of Nibiru and claim it to be the origin of their gods, the Anunnaki. They say this planet has a king; his name is Anu. Yes, we are saying "is"; the Nibiruians are mortal, but virtually deathless because of a concoction they take, something that comes from their planet.

According to Sitchin's translations, the atmosphere of Nibiru is slowly deteriorating. The Nibiruians were facing extinction if they didn't find a solution. The planet's scientists discovered that by adding ionized gold particles to their atmosphere, they were able to hold on to their existing atmospheric particles. They would need a lot of gold to accomplish this, more than could be found on their own planet.

Anu was facing political problems 448,000 years ago. He had a challenger to his authority named Alalu, but this challenger lost his bid to take power. Alalu fled the planet in a spaceship and landed here on Earth. He discovered that Earth had gold in large quantities. He saw this knowledge as a bargaining chip to return to Nibiru and re-ingratiate himself.

He was forgiven by Anu and this was when Anu found out that Earth was a source for their desperately needed gold. [137]

There are hundreds of examples of ancient artwork from all around the globe depicting what appear to be astronauts. Some notable examples include the sarcophagus lid of the Maya king Pakal the Great, who ruled in the sixth century A.D., which shows a man in what appears to be the cockpit of a space capsule. Inca clay figures found in Ecuador that were sculpted in 1,500 B.C. clearly show men in space suits. Japanese Dogu figurines carved in 1,200 B.C. look like humanoids in space suits. Petroglyphs from Val Camonica, Italy, clearly depict humanoids wearing glass helmets. The Native American Hopi and Zuni tribes' petroglyphs show the "star people" wearing space suits. The Man in Serpent sculpture by the Olmecs depicts a man sitting in a capsule manipulating levers. [129]

One of these astronaut sculptures is of the Sumerian goddess Inanna, also called Ishtar. The statue was found at the Mari excavation site along the Euphrates River. It depicts the goddess dressed as an astronaut with straps across her torso, a helmet, a neck box, ear phones and an oxygen hose running down her back. There are several depictions of Inanna as an astronaut and there are texts describing the seven accouterments necessary for her to don in order to fly. Inanna was said to be a lover of Anu's, which would entail frequent space voyages. [166]

According to Sitchin, the vehicle used by the Anunnaki to fly to heaven was called a "mu" or a "shem." In a hymn to Inanna/Ishtar about her travels, she has to wear special clothing.

Lady of Heaven;

She puts on the Garment of Heaven;

She valiantly ascends towards Heaven.

Over all the peopled lands she flies in her MU.

Lady, who in her MU to the heights of Heaven joyfully wings.

Over all the resting places she flies in her MU.

This is the type of language found in the Sumerian cuneiform tablets. They are clearly writing about special garments needed to fly in a spaceship that travels to Heaven. The Sumerian cuneiform symbol for MU looks like the nose of a space capsule. The Sumerian word ZAG. MU.KU translates to "high to heaven, bright at night." [137]

In the Sumerian story *The Epic of Gilgamesh,* the king of Uruk, Gilgamesh, goes on a quest to see if he can attain immortality. He is aware of several stories where mortals have been permitted to ascend to heaven. His plan therefore is to fly to heaven and become immortal or at least to extend his life. In the epic, he travels to the launching place of the shems, translated to "the place where the shems are raised up," which Sitchin believes is the base of the Temple of Jupiter at Baalbek, Lebanon. There he witnesses at close hand what sounds very much like a modern-day rocket launching.

The heavens shrieked, the earth boomed;

Daylight failed, darkness came.

Lightning flashed, a flame shot up.

The clouds swelled, it rained death!

Then the glow vanished; the fire went out.

All that had fallen had turned to ashes.

Anyone who has ever watched the space shuttle or any other large rocket launch, has seen the clouds swelling and the fire shooting up.

THE MANY NAMES OF THE ANUNNAKI

The Anunnaki change their names a lot. They are confusing to track and that is an understatement. They are called by different names whenever they move to new places, change jobs, become parents and attain new accomplishments, and they have been given different names by human populations in different countries.

For example, on Nibiru the sister of Enlil and Ea was Sud (which means nurse); when she became a mother on earth she was called Nin-mah with the nickname Mammu (Nammu) or "the mother"; in her capacity of medical officer in the early days of the colony she was called Ninti, meaning "lady of life; and" it wasn't until she relocated to the mountains of the southern Sinai Peninsula and became the ruler of the second spaceport that she was called Ninhursag, "lady of the mountain-head." Her Akkadian name was Belet-ili, "womb goddess." In the Greek pantheon she was Gaia, in Egypt her name was Hathor, and she was Cybele to Romans and Anatolians (central Turkey).

The various aliases of the main gods to which this book will be referring are listed in the chart below, but in this book we will be calling them by their Sumerian names and their appropriate aliases referenced as necessary. Sud is most frequently named Ninhursag.

The Sumerian Anunnaki Pantheon

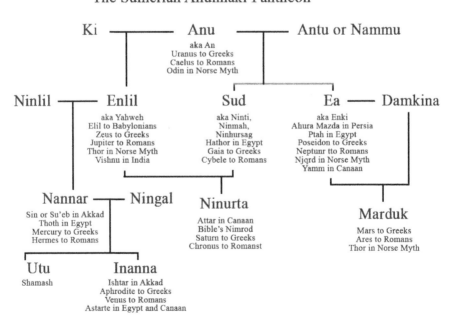

Their various aliases are also difficult to track. Ea's (or Enki's) son Marduk became the ruler of Babylon, and when he did so he rewrote himself in the role of the great hero god into the histories of that region. Enlil was usually cast in this role with his equivalent attributions being Zeus to the Greeks or Jupiter to the Romans, but due to Marduk's self-aggrandizement, we sometimes see him attributed as these two gods instead.

The Anunnaki and their works upon our world are a critically important part of our history, but the most important part of all was their relationship to the human race.

THE ANUNNAKI COME TO EARTH

The Anunnaki's interest in planet Earth began 448,000 years ago on their home planet of Nibiru.

Modern-day academia relegates the histories of these beings to myth and legend, but the Sumerian clay cuneiform tablets found in the ancient cities of Mesopotamia do not speak of the history of their gods as legend, but rather of documented history.

They speak of the year of their arrival, of their mandate, their place of origin, their early building projects, their motives for coming here, the purpose of their early cities and of their families and their relationships, all with alacrity, consistency and believability.

About 445,000 years ago, Anu sent his eldest son Ea to Earth to establish a colony and to try harvesting gold from Earth's oceans. Though Ea was Anu's eldest son, he was not his heir; his second son Enlil was his heir because Ea was born to Anu's wife, Antu, and Enlil was born to his half-sister, Ki. In the royal bloodlines of Nibiru, a son born of a half-sister had a higher rank than one born of a wife. A practice adopted by the Egyptian pharaohs on Earth.

Ea, which translates to "whose house is water," was a highly skilled engineer and scientist. He was therefore a very good choice to establish the Earth colony. When he came to Earth and began his building projects, he acquired his new name of Enki (lord of firm ground), and had a nickname of Nudinmud, which Sitchin translated as "he who made things." [137]

Let's briefly return to our made-up world of Tethus. In Chapter 9 we proposed the hypothetical scenario that we visited another planet and called it Tethus. There we found a primitive but intelligent alien species, and we decided to observe and study them in secret so as not to disturb them.

But, what would we have done differently if we desperately needed a valuable resource, like gold, from the planet? What if we were forced by circumstances into a situation where we had to exploit the planet?

In this situation we would not set up a duck blind to observe the natives; we would instead establish a colony there; we would begin importing workers to mine the gold and build our settlements. We wouldn't care if our presence disrupted the peace of the indigenous people; we would probably just shove them aside and take whatever land we needed for our purposes. Our desperate need would give us all the justification we required.

Essentially this was the same situation faced by the Nibiruians. Anu sent his eldest son, Ea, to establish a colony on Earth 443,000 years ago. Ea landed in the Persian Gulf and built the city of Eridu, aka Earth Station 1, at the southern end of Mesopotamia (modern-day Iraq), the land between the Tigris and Euphrates Rivers, also known as the Fertile Crescent and the cradle of civilization. The Nibiruians had become the Anunnaki, those who from heaven to Earth came, or more specifically those sent by Anu in heaven to Earth came.

In Sitchin's first book, he paints a picture of ancient Mesopotamia, and its effects on later history.

Some of the reasons Sitchin believed the Anunnaki chose the land of Mesopotamia as their first settlement were that the Earth was in the middle of an ice age at the time and choices of ice-free land were limited, that Mount Ararat was an excellent reference point easily visible from space, that the two large rivers would be a convenient source of water and transportation and also that there was easy access to bitumens as a ready and convenient fuel source. When they arrived on Earth, the area would have had pools of oil and fields of other bitumens literally laying on the surface, bubbling up from below the sands.

The use of petroleum products as a fuel, and other uses like asphalt roads, waterproofing, caulking and solvents, was described in Sumer in 3,500 B.C. [137]

In Mesopotamia, Enki built a spaceport at Sippar, a mission-control center at Nippur and a smelting center at Shuruppak. Gold was processed and air lifted to an orbiting station called the Igigi. Other Sumerian translations also refer to the Igigi as the Anunnaki gold miners.

Enki's sister, Sud, arrived on Earth 428,000 years ago along with a lot more colonists. She was the colony's chief medical officer and with the new job came her new name of Ninti, "lady life."

Enki had always been jealous of his brother Enlil, because even though he was the eldest brother he was not Anu's heir. [137]

This may have been the reason Enki strove so hard to become such a brilliant engineer and scientist. This brotherly enmity figured large in all their interactions on Earth and the following events helped to cement it in place.

The original plan of siphoning gold from Earth's oceans turned out to be too slow and didn't produce enough gold quickly enough to satisfy Anu, who with Enki's brother Enlil in tow, came to Earth himself 414,000 years ago. Anu put Enlil in charge of the Earth colony before returning to Nibiru, but Enlil did not rule the Earth alone; a council of the top twelve ranking Anunnaki ruled together and Enlil was at the head of this council.

Enki, supplanted as the head of the Earth colony, was sent to south-eastern Africa to set up gold mining operations at "the place of the waters," called the Abzu by the Anunnaki. The Abzu is associated with the Underworld of Greek mythology, not because it was underground, although there were certainly underground mines there, but just because it was far south in the Southern Hemisphere. In Sumerian texts the Abzu was said to be a beautiful place. Sitchin surmised that the Abzu was located near the Zambezi River, and in fact ancient mines have been discovered there dating back 50,000 years, and even older mines dating back 150,000 to 200,000 years have been found in South Africa.

Mainstream archaeology says no one is supposed to have been mining that many years ago, but the existence of these mines discredits those theories. [162] [167] [168]

There have also been recent discoveries of ancient mining sites in Peru that experts are dating to fifty thousand years ago. According to mainstream archaeology, humans didn't populate the Americas until about 20,000 years ago when they crossed the land bridge from Asia over the Bering Sea during the last ice age. This theory is on very shaky ground since there have been hundreds of discoveries that refute it, but again mainstream archaeology refuses to budge, even in the face of overwhelming evidence. [169]

More colonists were imported from Nibiru to become gold miners, and as is the case with most colonies, a disproportionate number of the colonists were male.

The Anunnaki miners staged a revolt 298,000 years ago. They did so when Enlil was visiting the mines and they surrounded his quarters, threatening his life. This enraged Enlil, who wanted to kill them, but the council of twelve determined that the work in the mines was too onerous and the miners had been justified in their revolt.

The Atrahasis is the Akkadian/Babylonian epic of the Great Flood. The Atrahasis tablets translated by Stephanie Dalley read, "When the gods instead of man did the work, bore the loads, the gods' load was too great, the work too hard, the trouble too much… They groaned and blamed each other, grumbled over the masses of excavated soil. 'Let us confront the chamberlains, and get him to relieve us of our hard work… They flared up. When they reached the gate of warrior Ellis's (Enlil's) dwelling, it was night, the middle watch, the house was surrounded… Every single one of us gods declared war! We have put a stop to the digging. The load is excessive, it is killing us!" [170]

How would we Earthlings have handled a similar situation on Tethus? Since transporting workers would be costly and time consuming, and since the work of gold mining is unpleasant and onerous, we would probably start exploiting the Tethans as slave labor.

But, what if the Tethans were not intelligent enough to do the work? At this point in our future technological development, we would probably have the ability to uplift their species using genetic engineering; we are already nearing the point when we could accomplish this now. If we did have the ability, we might start manipulating the Tethans' DNA, making them smarter, and then we might start breeding the newly improved model to be our gold-mining labor force.

The Anunnaki decided they needed a workforce. According to Sitchin, they gave the task of creating a worker, an adamu, or Adam, to Enki and Ninti. The Anunnaki did not create man out of nothing; they took specimens of Homo erectus and uplifted them into modern man, creating the first Homo sapiens.

Enki was one of the gods who spoke up on behalf of the workers, agreeing with them that the work was too hard and proposing a solution to the problem.

"Belet-ili (Ninti/Ninhursag) the womb goddess is present… Let her create primeval man, so that he may bear the yoke, so that he may bear the work of Ellil…let the womb goddess create offspring, and let man bear the load of the gods!"

Belet-ili essentially replied that she needed Enki's help to accomplish the creation: "[T]he work is Enki's; he makes everything pure! If he gives me clay, then I will do it."

Here we surmise that the "clay" Ninhursag is talking about is specimens of Homo erectus which Enki could provide to her from his controlled region of southern Africa.

Then Enki described the procedure for infusing the spirit of a slaughtered god into their creation: "I shall make a purification by washing. Then one god should be slaughtered. And the god can be purified by immersion. Ninti shall mix the clay with his flesh and blood. Then a god and a man will be mixed together in clay. Let us hear the drumbeat forever after, let a ghost come into existence from the god's flesh, let her proclaim it as his living sign."

After the work Ninti said, "I have carried out perfectly the work that you ordered of me. You have slaughtered a god together with his intelligence. I have relieved you of your hard work, I have imposed your load on man." [170]

In another passage translated by Sitchin, Ea spoke of the connection between blood and the soul:

In the clay, god and man shall be bound,

to a unity brought together;

So that to the end of days

The flesh and the soul

Which in a god have ripen,

That soul in a blood-kinship be bound. [170]

In his first book, Sitchin said, "The Nephilim took an ape-man and implanted on him their own image and likeness.... The ovum of a female Homo erectus, fertilized by the genes of a god, was then implanted within the womb of Ea's spouse; and after the "model" was obtained, duplicates of it were implanted in the wombs of birth goddesses, to undergo the process of pregnancy and birth."

They were using their own DNA in their uplifting, or creation, of mankind.

When Darwin wrote his *On the Origin of Species* book, it set off a controversial battle between the scientific community and the church. The scientists argued that of course man evolved just like all the other creatures on the planet. The church defended the Bible story that man was created by God. How crazy is it that both sides might have been right?

If the story of the Anunnaki uplifting early man is true, then our human ancestors gradually and naturally evolved into Homo erectus, and were then uplifted by the Anunnaki into Homo sapiens. If this did happen, then it is also true that the "gods" created man, as is described in the Bible. We weren't created from scratch; the gods just put the finishing touches on us, skipping ahead over what would have had to be about a million more years of evolution.

Sitchin believed this uplifting was the explanation for the missing link between Homo erectus and Homo sapien. There is a drastic difference in the brain sizes of these two hominids. [171] [172]

Homo sapiens have the power of speech; no other primates including Homo erectus were supposed to have had this ability. The speech centers in our DNA seem to be an addition to our code spliced in by our uplifters. There is no precursor to the speech centers of our brain in any primate species, no developmental early stages like there are for all our other senses. There are early versions of scent, sight, hearing, all the senses, but not speech.

In one Sumerian text, the being modified by the Anunnaki is described:

When mankind was created,

They knew not the eating of bread,

Knew not the dressing in garments;

Ate plants with their mouth like sheep;

Drank water from a ditch.

In a relatively short amount of time, our brains went through an intense amount of change. We evolved from animal-like beasts lapping water out of streams on all fours, to reasoning beings creating cups to drink from; aware of our nakedness, we started wearing clothing. In a period of about 60,000 years we skipped about one million years ahead in evolution.

The globalization, or new globular shape of the human brain, which is different from its predecessors, allowed for the rapid expansion of the cerebellum and the development of the frontal cortex, which increased coordination, logic, short- and long-term memory and spatial and critical thinking, and allowed for the development of the language centers.

Prior to this expansion it took a million years for ape-like creatures to start walking upright and another million to become tool users; then suddenly, we were able to represent objects in our world symbolically, able to think abstractly, able to draw images of the animals in our environment as representatives of the real thing. Abstract thinking abilities are the necessary seeds of developing a spoken language, and are the thing that most sets us apart from all other intelligent animals on the Earth.

The uplift theory also explains why the existence of Homo erectus and Homo sapien overlapped each other. Instead of slowly and gradually evolving from one to the other, a small group separated into a much more highly advanced specimen, eventually squeezing the inferior one out and replacing them.

According to the Sumerian records, the Anunnaki set about breeding their new creation and putting them to work in the mines of Africa.

The early versions of mankind, known as the Adamic race, were longer lived than we are now, with lifespans of about one thousand years. There is a passage in the book of Genesis that says God decided to set the human lifespan to 120 years around the time of Moses.

At first Enki jealously guarded his creation, keeping human laborers to himself and his African mining operations. Enlil coveted these workers, wanting to have some of them to work in the Mesopotamian settlements. Enki resisted sharing us with his brother. Enlil then conducted a raid on the mines, breaking into the underworld and stealing human workers away.

Over the ensuing 290,000 years, the history of Sumeria tells that the Anunnaki ruled the region themselves, continuing with their gold mining, processing and shipping projects, and expanding their mining efforts into other parts of the world. They also continued with their uplifting project, improving their Homo sapien into Homo sapien sapien, or the current version of modern man.

The king's list of Sumeria shows various Anunnaki kings ruling for many thousands of years each. One king ruled for about 43,000 years, indicating that these were the Anunnaki themselves.

The king's list of ancient Egypt also shows very long reigns of their early kings. Ptah ruled for nine thousand years and Ra after him ruled for one thousand years. Ptah was said to be a master builder who constructed enormous dykes to stop the flooding of the Nile. We believe Ptah was another name for Enki and Ra was Marduk. [137]

Around 50,000 years ago, Enlil began to hate mankind. We believe that this was partly because his brother Enki co-created them, and along with their sister Ninhursag, favored them, and partly because of something else that happened.

During this time period, the Anunnaki had spread their sphere of influence into Canaan territory (modern day Israel, Jordan, Syria and Lebanon), into Egypt, India and the Mediterranean and later into the New World, and wherever the Anunnaki went, they brought their human slaves with them.

The colony did not have an even male to female ratio, and the Anunnaki began taking wives from the human race and having children by them. Most scholars call these children the Nephilim, though Sitchin considered the Anunnaki and the Nephilim to be the same creatures.

Whichever of these distinctions is true, it is clear that the Old Testament, the book of Enoch and the ancient Sumerian texts describe a situation where alien beings were mating with human women and producing offspring.

The Old Testament is clear on this point:

"The sons of the gods saw the daughters of man, that they were good; and they took them for wives."

"The Nephilim were upon the Earth, in those days and thereafter too, when the sons of the gods cohabitated with the daughters of the Adam, and they bore children unto them."

The skeleton of a high-ranking woman, Queen Puabi, was discovered by British archaeologist Sir Charles Leonard Woolley in 1922 in the royal cemetery of Ur. This woman is said to be a first-dynasty queen from around 2,600 B.C. She has a very unusual, large, misshapen head, and Sitchin believed she was one of these hybrid beings. Sitchin pushed for her remains to be DNA tested to support his theories, but to no avail; the Natural History Museum of London continued to refuse to do the testing.

This mating is supposed to have been possible because of the sharing of the waters when the planets Nibiru and Tiamat collided with one another, and the seeds of life were shared between them. This water sharing was supposed to be the reason for the two planets' evolving similar life-forms. Apparently there were creatures similar to Homo erectus that also evolved on Nibiru. According to the author Gerald Clark, Enki stated that the bipedal hominids he found on the African plains were recognizable as a species based on the evolutionary process seen on Nibiru. [111]

It could also have been the case that Enki, always striving against his brother's wishes, was helping to facilitate the production of these hybrid beings. He certainly had the necessary genetic manipulation skills.

Enlil viewed this interbreeding as both disgusting and blasphemous. In his rage, he expelled all his human workers from his garden estate in Mesopotamia called ED.IN. Here we have the origin of the story of the expulsion of Adam and Eve from the Garden of Eden.

The Sumerian version of the story makes more sense to us. The pair was supposedly expelled because they had eaten from the tree of knowledge. The Biblical meaning of "knowledge" is sexual "knowing." Why would a god forbid a human from having sex with another human or for that matter, why would he be angry if they ate an apple? It doesn't seem likely, but he might be plenty angry at the idea of other gods mating with humans. That may indeed have been considered a blasphemy in the eyes of Enlil.

In the biblical story it was said to be a snake that spoke to Eve and convinced her to break God's command. In Sumerian texts Enki is often associated with a snake. We believe this is further proof of Enki's hand in facilitating the breeding of the demigods that so enraged his brother Enlil.

The Anunnaki are frequently depicted as being much larger than humans. These hybrid beings were said to be gigantic in stature and much more powerful than the average human, and also longer lived. There are many stories about these demigods in Greek mythology.

Sitchin marks this time as the beginning of Enlil's enmity against humans and there are stories about him causing famines and illnesses among the humans to cull their numbers and reduce their "noise." During this time human populations were reduced to scattered hunter gatherers, barely scratching out their existence, except for the workers of Enki still mining for gold.

Enlil stewed over his dislike of humans for quite some time before judgment day came.

Sitchin thought that about 13,000 years ago the Anunnaki realized the South Pole ice sheet had become unstable and was about to shift due to the imminent passage of Nibiru through the solar system. But Sitchin, who died in 2010, did not know about the Hiawatha Asteroid.

He believed the Anunnaki were not responsible for the Great Flood, but that Enlil's dislike of the humans caused him to order all the Anunnaki to keep humanity in the dark concerning their imminent destruction. His plan was for the gods to take off in their spaceships and watch the destruction from the safety of space.

Here we disagree with Sitchin's supposition. We believe Enlil resolved to destroy mankind and all these half-breed children. We believe he purposely chucked the Hiawatha Asteroid at Earth. There are many references in early religious writings that specifically say it was God's plan to destroy mankind and the Nephilim with the Great Flood.

We concede that it's possible that the Anunnaki didn't actually cause the Hiawatha Asteroid to hit Earth, and maybe they just spotted it coming instead, but the Sumerian tablets are clear about Enlil's deliberately keeping mankind in the dark about their coming demise.

In the Sumerian history, Enki defied his brother's order and resolved to warn mankind. We believe that it was Enki's voice heard warning about the imminent flood to the separate cultures, including the Sumerian's version of Noah, Ziusudra. We also believe that Enki may have protected his miners from the flood by sealing them deep underground in the various Anunnaki gold mines.

The book of Enoch explains the deluge story differently than does the book of Genesis. In the book of Genesis, God has decided to destroy mankind because of man's sins. The book of Enoch tells of God's anger being against the Nephilim and the deluge is perpetrated to destroy them and to rid mankind of the atrocities being perpetrated on them by the Nephilim.

Supposedly upon returning to Earth after the flood and discovering that Enki had defied him and helped some humans to survive, Enlil was angry, but was persuaded by the Anunnaki council to forgive both Enki and the surviving humans. He ended up making peace with Ziusudra and his family after the deluge because they were "pure" humans who did not engage in sex with the rebellious Anunnaki, and maybe also because they still needed a workforce to mine their gold.

After the Great Flood, all of the great cities of the Anunnaki were destroyed and nearly all the humans were killed, except for a few thousand survivors.

Enlil may have felt guilty for the flood, so he gave the human survivors a boost by giving them what they needed to form settlements and become farmers. We believe the gods gave man genetically engineered cereal grains and animals to help them.

In *The 12th Planet* Sitchin wrote, "Scholars, who have now established that agriculture began with the domestication of wild emmer as a source of wheat and barley, are unable to explain how the earliest grains were already uniform and highly specialized. Thousands of generations of genetic selection are needed by nature to acquire even a modest degree of sophistication. Yet the period, time or location in which such a gradual and very prolonged process might have taken place on Earth are nowhere to be found."

According to Sitchin mankind was in a state of regression between 27,000 and 11,000 B.C. with our population and civilization dwindling to almost a state of non-habitation (possibly being caused by Enlil's persecution). When suddenly, "thinking man reappeared with new vigor and on an inexplicably higher cultural level," changing from wandering hunter gatherers into farmers and shepherds.

For many years we suspected there was something to do with genetic engineering and the domesticated animals used by mankind. We wondered why there were so many varieties of domesticated animals but such a limited variety of wild ones. Why are there only two types of lion, but seventy-five breeds of domestic cat, why two elephants, but three hundred types of horse, why seven types of giraffe but one thousand breeds of cattle, why five species of rhino, but two hundred different breeds of goat, why thirty-five breeds of wild dog and over three hundred breeds of domestic dog? We didn't believe it just all came down to breeding. How do you breed a wolf into a Chihuahua?

It has always seemed as if the animals given to man as his own had somehow been modified to be malleable and easy to breed into different varieties. We believe the Anunnaki provided mankind with these gifts for more successful agriculture, to provide a food source for both the humans and themselves.

After the flood waters receded, we think a representative Anunnaki, or possibly their Adamic human/hybrid slaves, were deployed to each of the surviving human populations all around the world, helping them to recreate their civilization just as is described in almost all of the hundreds of flood myths where a "god" flies in and teaches them things. In our opinion, this was done in order to give man a boost, settling him into communities and then into civilizations.

The Anunnaki began rebuilding cities all around the planet in order to start their gold mining operations again.

The Egyptians believed their god Osirus came to them to teach them how to construct a civilization.

The Inca legends talk about their god Viracocha, a very tall, light-skinned, white-haired being, who appeared to them after the flood, rising out of Lake Titicaca. He taught them astronomy, agriculture and other advanced arts.

The Maya civilization believed their god Kukulkan taught them writing, mathematics and science.

We believe that whenever the Anunnaki expanded their mining operations into new locations, they would first build a pyramid power plant to have the necessary power to build a gold processing city. They would move a population of miners to the area, work the site until the gold was all but gone and then move on to a new site.

Sitchin makes a convincing case that it was the Anunnaki who expanded their gold mining operations into Mesoamerica and the west coast countries of South America.

He said Enki first brought his South African workers to Mesoamerica, which is why the giant heads of the Olmecs have features reminiscent of some South African peoples.

The Peruvian, Ecuadorian and Bolivian settlements were populated from the Mesopotamian slave stock and so these people do resemble the ancient peoples of that region.

When viewed as possible gold mining operations, a lot of the mysteries of the megalithic constructions of these American cities start to make sense. The zig-zagging walls of Sacsayhuaman could be huge sluicing stations for separating gold from muddy water funneled into them. This could be why the walls were tilted inward and sloped downward, to support the pressure of huge amounts of water funneling through them, and why no mortar was used, since it would have been washed away. The reason for placing these cities at high elevations starts to make more sense. That's where most of the gold would be, inside the mountains of the region. It makes sense why complex aqueducts were constructed to these cities, even when a supply of fresh water was readily available. They weren't bringing in drinking water, they were running huge quantities of water in to separate out the gold and prepare it for transport. [166]

There is one piece of hard evidence proving there was a Sumerian connection to the new world. The Fuente Magna bowl is a large ceramic bowl with Sumerian cuneiform writing and proto-Sumerian hieroglyphs carved into it. The bowl was found by a farmer in the 1950s near Lake Titicaca in Peru. It is estimated to be five thousand years old.

There are many stories worldwide about the "gods" arriving, building cities and spawning a population of humans, and then later these humans disappearing without a trace. We believe they didn't disappear, they were simply relocated to a different mining operation.

The Olmec dominated the area of La Venta, what is now modern-day Vera Cruz, for one thousand years before mysteriously disappearing around 300 B.C.

The Nazca people disappeared about 800 A.D.

The Maya vanished around 900 A.D.

In the Mesopotamian region in the years after the flood, the Anunnaki began ruling more and more in absentia, through an upper class of humans, a priest/king class, frequently supposed to be part Anunnaki hybrids.

Where did the Anunnaki go after the Great Flood? We believe the Great Flood is a demarcation point. Prior to the flood, the Anunnaki lived among the humans and ruled the planet themselves. Post flood they let the human kings and priest class run their cities as long as they were loyal and worshiped them in temples built specifically for the worship of their in-absentia gods. We believe the Anunnaki themselves were establishing mining operations in other parts of the world and building underground bases.

We also believe that a large number of the gods returned to Nibiru after the flood; they were no longer needed as mining labor, and we believe the harshness of Enlil's punishment disheartened them.

It has been said that the Anunnaki were not comfortable on our planet, that it was not a healthy environment for them. This may also be a good reason for many of them to have left and another reason for the remaining gods to move underground.

Enlil, Enki and the other gods were described as returning to Mesopotamia to handle problems and conflicts that interfered with their projects. Where were they returning from?

Post flood, the Sumerian king's list begins to show human lifespans and reigns of kings, not of thousands of years but of decades.

According to Sitchin, the Anunnaki decided to change the location of the spaceport to the central plain of the Sinai Peninsula. The previous spaceport was located in Mesopotamia, as was their mission control center, but these facilities had been completely destroyed by the flood. The Anunnaki had previously used Mount Ararat as an easy-to-spot reference point to help them triangulate their ships to land at the spaceport in Mesopotamia.

The new spaceport had Mount Katherine at the southern end of the Sinai as one reference, but they needed another triangulation point and another mission control center. For these purposes, Enki, the master engineer and builder, was instructed to build the three highly advanced pyramids at the Giza Plateau to function as beacons to guide their spaceships to the Sinai spaceport and to also function as a mission control center. All of the other, more inferior pyramids in Egypt were built by the human pharaohs in later years, in their attempts to emulate the achievements of the gods. The Giza pyramids were built about 12,800 years ago after their original settlements in Mesopotamia were destroyed by the Great Flood.

We've noted the Sumerian interest in the zodiac, which plays an important part in their art. For instance, Enki is sometimes depicted as being a man with a fish tail and other times with streams full of swimming fish next to him. We believe this is the case not because he was really a half fish, but instead the astrological time of Pisces has particular significance for him in some way.

This may also be why Enlil is so closely associated with the "heavenly bull," that the Age of Taurus had particular significance for him. Sitchin thought it was Enlil's establishment of the city of Nippur as a mission control center, which happened in the Age of Taurus. Enlil named the city NIBRU.KI, which Sitchin translated as "Earth's crossing."

We think it possible that a similar consideration was taken when choosing a lion for the body of the Sphinx. The time period to which Sitchin attributed the building of the Giza complex would have been at the beginning of the Age of Leo the lion, which began about 10,800 B.C.

Sitchin also agreed with our assessment of the forgeries of Col. Vyse when he attributed the Great Pyramid to the pharaoh Khufu. In his book, *The Wars of Gods and Men*, he accuses Vyse and his assistants of forging the names found in the pyramid. In his books, he makes a compelling case that the Great Pyramid and the whole Giza site was built many thousands of years before Pharaoh Khufu.

Sitchin devoted his life's work to the translating of the great cuneiform libraries of the ancient Mesopotamians, and while mainstream academia has labeled him as a promoter of pseudoscience, we would much rather take the word of this brilliant scholar over that of a charlatan like Vyse.

Enki is the most obvious candidate to be the builder of the Giza complex. He and his son Marduk, to whom he taught his building skills, were most likely the architects of all the impossible megalithic structures of the ancient world.

Enlil refused to allow Enki to rule the area around the spaceport even though Africa was his domain, so the two brothers agreed to give rulership of the spaceport and the lower Nile region to their sister Ninti, who they both considered to be a neutral party. She moved to the mountains of the south Sinai at Mount Katherine. With the change of address and her new kingdom, Ninti had another name change, becoming Ninhursag (lady of the mountainhead). The spaceport was critically important to them not only because of the gold transporting necessity, but also because if any one faction controlled the spaceport, that faction would have control of access to the concoction the Anunnaki used to extend their lifespans.

Sitchin said Enki built the base of the Temple of Jupiter as a landing pad, explaining the "impossible" 880-ton trilithon stones in the structure.[137]

If the megalithic temples of Sardinia and Malta were actually built 12,000 years ago, they must have been built by Enki and Marduk. They were the only ones capable of building these megalithic structures at this time period. This supposition is supported by the fact that there are similarities between the Sardinian and Sumerian languages.

As the great Anunnaki became more preoccupied elsewhere, the lower ranking gods, ambitious in their own right, started to wage campaigns to seize power for themselves.

Enlil, Ninurta and their allies were in constant conflict with Enki, Marduk and their allies.

In these detailed and well researched histories, Sitchin makes a point about the humanlike characteristics of the "gods" and their very ungodlike behaviors.

The Anunnaki display many of the seven deadly sins with a few extra sins on top. They are jealous, vain, ridiculously proud, selfish, ambitious, intemperate, rash, lustful, slothful, grouchy, wrathful, vengeful and scheming. Their many character flaws, coupled with their far superior technology, inevitably lead to very warlike behavior for which they rarely suffered the consequences themselves. These are the last people anyone would want to have high technology like spaceflight and nuclear weapons.

In the conflicts between the two main sides, nuclear weapons were used in at least three instances: the destruction of Sodom and Gomorrah, the destruction of Mohenjo Daro in the Indus Valley and the destruction of the spaceport of the Sinai Peninsula. Sitchin places the annihilation of the spaceport in 2,024 B.C. and he says that the winds blew the radioactive cloud over Mesopotamia, making the people sick, the soil sterile and the area unlivable. So ended the Anunnaki's reign in the Fertile Crescent.

Sitchin said the cities of Sodom and Gomorrah were located on the shores of the Dead Sea and are now underwater there, and the waters of the sea are showing residual radioactivity.

Mohenjo Daro has obvious signs of a radioactive blast; walls and foundations are fused together. There is radioactive ash at the site with radioactive skeletons lying all around the town. The area was still being worked by human hands in 2,500 B.C., putting its possible destruction within five hundred years of the destruction of the Sinai spaceport.

Many scholars contend the destruction of Mohenjo Daro correlates to the wars described in the "Drona Parva" section of the Sanskrit epic the *Mahabharata*. The weapons used in the epic were described as, "A single projectile charged with all the power in the Universe…. An incandescent column of smoke and flame as bright as 10,000 suns, rose in all its splendor … it was an unknown weapon, an iron thunderbolt, a gigantic messenger of death which reduced to ashes an entire race." This sounds like a very good description of a nuclear blast. Survivors were said to have lost their hair and fingernails, symptoms of radiation sickness, and the food supply of the area was polluted. [133][173]

The destruction of the Sinai spaceport marks the end of Sitchin's third book, *The Wars of Gods and Men*. In the book's epilogue, Sitchin said that Enki and Marduk, using their advanced scientific knowledge, undertook the cleanup of the radiation in Sumer; he "cured the afflicted, purified the waters and made the soil grow edible vegetation again." Which may explain why the area is not still irradiated. [174]

We realize how nuts this all sounds, but if you think about it, this supposition solves a lot of mysteries. It answers the questions of why there are so many ancient pyramids all over the world that look to be constructed by the same builders. It explains the impossible megalithic constructions attributed to relatively primitive humans. It explains why the older a structure is, the more advanced it is. It explains why the human brain evolved so quickly. It explains the instant development of the highly advanced Sumerian society. It explains why the Earth's moon is so large and why the moon is the same mineral content of Earth. It explains where the asteroid belt came from. It explains the bizarre orbit of Pluto. It explains the gravitational perturbations of Uranus and Neptune. It explains why sophisticated genetically modified grains were grown by early humans.

If this is all true, then it might also explain who is buzzing our skies in highly advanced UFOs.

There may be a contingent of Anunnaki living under our feet, with their favored, advanced human slaves, and a population of Grey and Reptilian slave workers created for mining gold and running errands around the planet. If it is really they who are in residence, they are far more advanced than we are and they are continuing with their uplifting project, which is why they continue to kidnap human beings. They may also be taking humans as mates. When they retreated underground, they took populations of cattle and sheep with them as a food source. This is why they do cattle and sheep mutilations: they need DNA from surface animals to continue the viability of their herds.

One good reason for them to move their projects underground is that's where the gold is, underground.

Another good reason why the Anunnaki may have moved into underground settlements is because they do not enjoy living on the surface of our world. The only time Nibiru is in proximity to a bright sun is when it passes through our solar system between Mars and Jupiter. Our sun would appear much smaller and far less bright when viewed from Nibiru at this apogee of their orbit. When they came to our planet, the sun would be brighter and hotter than anything they ever experienced on Nibiru. We surmise that the Nibiruians would feel quite uncomfortable in the intensity of our noon-day sun. We surmise that this might have been why they built the ziggurats in Mesopotamia, which they described as "a house that is a mountain." These giant houses have very few windows. The Anunnaki could have resided inside these huge palaces during the day and emerged at night for their various outdoor activities.

THE ANUNNAKI ALIEN THEORY IS MORE PLAUSIBLE

If aliens really are involved at all, we believe Sitchin's theories are more plausible than most other visiting alien theories.

Most theories floating around the world of ufology refer to the aliens flying UFOs in our skies as "visitors" from another solar system.

Other theories propose these aliens are traveling here from our own future, presuming a theoretical time machine to be possible.

Many alien visitor theories claim they are coming here so frequently because they can easily do so. They are coming here via wormholes or portals or using crafts that can move at faster-than-light speeds. Sure these things might be possible, especially if the alien civilization is millions of years more advanced than we are, but Sitchin's theory (with which we agree) does not have to take the problems of time dilation and the limitations of mass moving near the speed of light into account.

So far, no wormholes have been detected. In Sitchin's theory, no theoretical wormhole is needed and nothing so grandiose as space folding or time machines is being proposed. The Anunnaki who came here 445,000 years ago were using good old fashioned rocketry-based space travel. The massive distances of interstellar space travel do not apply in this case. The enormous orbit of Nibiru brings this planet close enough to ours so that light-speed travel is not necessary. The work of crossing these great distances is handled by the planet's natural orbit.

We think this makes Sitchin's theories of extraterrestrial visitation much, much more plausible than believing a race from a distant star system is visiting us so frequently they are spotted 10,000 times per year. Nibiru cruises by every 3,600 years like a regular commuter train. It's easy for the Anunnaki to schedule their arrivals, immigrate to our planet for a tour of duty, and then return home with another shipment of gold when the planet swings by again.

This time frame would not be arduously long for the Anunnaki because of their nearly deathless lifespans. They are never in a hurry by our standards. Enlil's anger against mankind percolated for about 37,000 years before he decided to let mankind be destroyed.

It was Sitchin who discovered that the length of the Anunnaki reigns on the Sumerian king's list correspond exactly to multiples of 3,600 the length of a single orbit of Nibiru, i.e., Alulim ruled for 28,800, which is

3,600 times eight; Alalgar ruled for 36,000 years, which is ten times; En-menluanna ruled for 43,200 years, which is twelve times; and so on. [137]

Hiawatha's impact did a good job of erasing our past. The known history of the world pretty much stops 13,000 years ago and goes back no further. The one-thousand-foot-tall tsunami literally scraped it off the surface of the world.

Graham Hancock wrote in his book *Fingerprints of the Gods*, "...our species could have been afflicted with some terrible amnesia and that the dark period so blithely and dismissively referred to as 'prehistory' might turn out to conceal unimagined truths about our own past." We fully concur. [111]

Human beings have played a significant part in our own history erasure over the years, having burned the libraries at Alexandria and Constantiople and destroyed all the ancient texts of the Americas with early Christian zealotry, and whatever secrets the Vatican might be hiding in their library, well, they aren't telling.

There are almost no records preceding the impact of Hiawatha, but the exception is the Royal Library of Ashurbanipal.

The ancient Sumerians suffered no such amnesia, but their history tells such a fantastic story that scholars translating them wrote the whole history off as myth and legend, instead of the factual account Sitchin believed it to be.

WHAT DO THE ANUNNAKI LOOK LIKE?

There are many depictions of the Anunnaki gods and kings where they appear to be humans. One of the strange things about them, though, is they all seem to be identical twins. They all look exactly alike and in order to tell them apart, the translation of inscriptions or symbols near them is needed. It's almost as if they all donned human-faced masks to interact with the people of Earth.

Studying carvings of Anunnaki gods gives a feeling that they may be wearing human masks. It is impossible to tell the gods apart from each other without the help of inscriptions or identifying symbols on the carvings. Photo credits: iStock.

In ancient Mesopotamia, artifacts were unearthed by Sir Leonard Woolley leading an excavation to uncover the remains of one of the oldest agriculture communities in the world, the Ubaid culture, dating back to 5,900 B.C. or about eight thousand years ago. He found weird clay figurines that appear to have Reptilian facial features, perhaps the real Anunnaki, with elongated skulls and lizard eyes and pig-like noses. These figurines are breast feeding, like mammalians do. The eyes are very large but hooded, appearing to be open in narrow slits.

The Ant People of the Hopi are taller and broader-shouldered than humans with very large eyes and what appear to be antennae.

Some early Anunnaki statues have human-like faces with huge, staring eyes. [175]

Many ufologist theories say aliens came here, built a bunch of impossible structures and then left. Maybe this is true, or maybe, as we propose, some of them never left. They are still here, still enacting their agenda, still uplifting humanity and still mining for gold deep inside the Earth's crust.

Sitchin believed in another possible hidden base of the Anunnaki. He believed they may be mining gold on Mars. It makes sense. Nibiru passes through the gap between Mars and Jupiter. Mars would have been a much closer source of gold, though the conditions would have been much more difficult to endure.

About one billion years ago Mars lost its magnetic field. A planet's magnetic field is generated by the liquid mantle moving over the core. It's a smaller planet than Earth and its mantle cooled faster. With no magnetic field, the solar wind from the sun bombarded the planet and slowly ripped off its atmosphere. Mars now has only about one percent of its atmosphere left. [176]

Mars' atmosphere appears to have also been damaged by the impact of a Chixulube-size meteor which created the Lyot Impact Basin about half a billion years ago. [177]

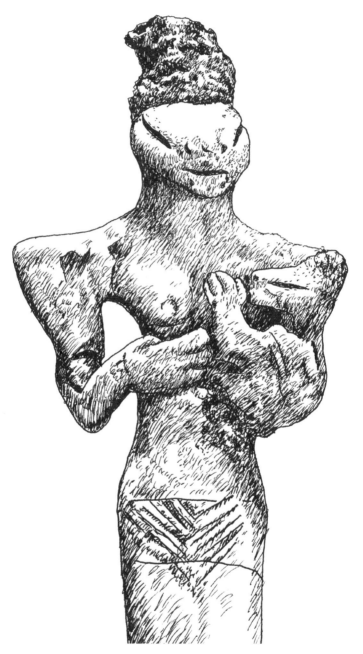

This strange sculpture comes from the Ubaid region of Mesopotamia. It depicts a figure with weird lizard-like features, but is breast feeding like a lactating mammal. It has been dated to roughly 7000 years old. Drawing by Leslie Shaw.

The Anunnaki were more technologically advanced 445,000 years ago than we are now. They would have been able to overcome the difficulties of mining on Mars.

The site of Cydonia is the region where the face on Mars is, and next to it there is a complex of pyramidal structures. One of the pyramids is five-sided, and this is not supposed to be something that occurs in nature.

The face on Mars would have aligned perfectly with the sunrise of Mars's equinox 225,000 years ago, and the Anunnaki were famous for building astronomical alignments into their structures. If they did build this site that long ago, it would explain the severe weathering suffered by the site; Mars has fierce storms.

If the site is really an artificial construct, then this goes a long way to proving the Anunnaki's presence in our solar system. While mainstream archaeology continues to frustratingly attribute the ancient structures on Earth to primitive people, they would be hard pressed to do so with a site on Mars. [177]

There is another piece of evidence pointing to the Anunnaki's activities on Mars. The planet has two spots with very high radiation signatures, at Mare Acidalium and Utopia Planum. These two nuclear hotspots are very close to the site at Cydonia. At first it was thought that these might be natural radioactive places, but closer examination proved this was not the case. The xenon isotopes in particular point to weapons-grade nuclear signatures. The xenon isotope spectrum indicates a fast neutron event, not a moderated reaction. The Lyot Impact Basin is also very close to the Cydonia site.

The physicist John E Brandenburg, who authored three books on Mars, concluded that the nuclear signatures on Mars could only have been created by nuclear weapons. [178]

We believe Sitchin was right and the Anunnaki set up mining operations on Mars at some point in the past, but Sitchin didn't know about the underground bases here on Earth. He believed the UFOs in our skies were advanced scout ships of the Anunnaki coming from Nibiru or were possibly visiting ships from their base on Mars.

CHAPTER SIXTEEN

THE CONTINUED BREEDING PROGRAM

We've described the Anunnaki as in desperate and constant need of gold. They literally need it for the continued survival of life on their planet. If this is true, then their need for gold will be unending, and they will have to continue mining it from other planets forever.

Mankind has always been fascinated by and covetous of gold, more than any other metal. It's possible we were influenced to this covetousness from our contact with the Anunnaki and by their use of us to mine it.

The Anunnaki bred us as a slave worker race, but this relationship may not have been ideal for them. It's possible that when the Anunnaki created the modern human race, they made us too much like themselves, with many of their own faults built in.

Maybe, as we said in the "Meet the Tethans" chapter, humans are difficult to use as a slave race. We are an unruly, willful bunch and don't take to slavery well. Perhaps the Greys are the Anunnaki's next slave model, emotionless, unambitious and not prone to rebellion or willfulness.

Greys are described as cookie-cutter beings, all alike. They are able to communicate with us telepathically. If something is able to communicate with us telepathically, then perhaps we can presume them to be of similar ancestry with similar brains?

Abductees sometimes describe their abductors as very human-like. We think these are the "Nordic aliens" who share common ancestors with modern man, but who separated their race from ours in the past.

They also communicate with their abductees through telepathy and are able to read our minds. It was these aliens who waylaid Admiral Byrd to give him their message for President Truman.

We believe that the humans who accompanied the Anunnaki into their underground bases are members of the Adamic race. They are taller than we are, they are longer lived and with the Anunnaki as their teachers, they are far more technologically advanced than we are.

Remote viewers who have "visited" alien bases have later been tracked back to their homes and had aliens appear in their bedrooms. They are able to sense when they are being observed by remote viewers. When flying in their UFOs, they are also able to sense when humans are observing them. Witnesses frequently report UFOs "reacting" to being seen.

We believe there is a pecking order in these underground alien communities. The Anunnaki are at the top of course, their Adamic-race humans are next, and then their more recent creations, the Greys and Reptilians, are on the lower rung. We believe the Greys and Reptilians have been bred by the Anunnaki to largely replace human slaves as laborers.

We think most of the Anunnaki have returned to Nibiru and have left their Adamic-race humans in charge of their Earth-based projects. So if this is true, ironically, most of the aliens are gone, and the remaining people flying in the UFOs are Earthlings, born and bred. Just as we surface dwellers are hybrids of Homo erectus and the Anunnaki races, so are the people living within our planet, though their percentage of Anunnaki DNA may be higher than ours.

Remote viewers have also said they've seen advanced humans performing experiments on regular people, so it seems the breeding program is being conducted by the Adamic humans now.

As was evidenced by Travis Walton's testimony, the Greys and the human-like Nordic aliens are fellow crew members on the larger "motherships," proving themselves to be working together, and disabusing the theory that they are completely separate alien species coming here from two different planets. The smaller scout ships that have crashed to Earth from time to time never (as far as we know) have the Nordic aliens on them. We think this proves the Greys are not much more than errand runners for the Nordics, who we believe created them as a slave species. [72]

As we've said before, some of the changes in the slave model could have taken place naturally. What would humans look like if we were taken underground for 13,000 years? We might become smaller, grayer, the size of our eyes might grow and the size of our pupils expand until the whole eye appears black.

They may also have become more sickly and maybe they need DNA from healthy surface dwellers to keep their slave races viable.

Another race of "aliens" has been reported by abductees: the Reptilians. If the Anunnaki needed a Reptilian race of workers for certain types of aquatic work, why not just engineer them? They wouldn't need to create them from scratch; just take your Grey model and modify them. Humans have Reptilian DNA in our genetic code; it may be as simple as pulling this part of our DNA and repurposing it.

There is yet another alien race reported by abductees called the Insectoids. They appear to be Grey aliens with distorted proportions making them look mantis-like. We think they are another hybrid variation.

We also know from Phil Schneider's testimony that Greys and Reptilians are working together at the Dulce Air Force Base. We believe they are not members of separate, visiting alien races working together in some galactic Federation. We instead believe they are hybrid variations on a theme, bred as workers for the Nordics. They may be lying about this in an effort to keep us looking up, when we really should be looking down.

Professor David M. Jacobs, an historian and retired associate professor of history at Temple University, has authored five books on the subject of alien abductions. He is famous in ufology circles, has taught classes in the UFO phenomenon for about 25 years and has lectured widely on the subject.

In his research, mostly utilizing hypnotic regression, he has documented many thousands of abduction events. Many of these victims are women who report stolen fetuses. They are impregnated during an abduction, and about four months later are abducted again and the fetus is removed. There has been ultrasound evidence of some of these pregnancies and follow-up ultrasounds documenting the missing fetuses. The women's wombs do not appear to have suffered miscarriages. They are completely devoid of tissue, which is not usually the case in miscarriages – as if their uteruses had been vacuumed out.

Many of these women claim to have been introduced to their hybrid children during subsequent abductions. Sometimes the women report this abuse taking place several times, with all their children stolen away. [179]

From his long years of research, Jacobs has theorized the aliens are using these hybrid children for a covert program of infiltration of human society.

He also claims these human hybrids have a distinct advantage over their regular human counterparts: they are able to read our minds. We believe both these suppositions to be true.

Jacobs says these abductions are handled expeditiously, and efficiently and seem to be very goal driven. The aliens "never stand around wondering what to do next." They take the people they want, get the samples they want and return the abductees. Many abductees report missing time of around forty minutes; expeditious indeed.

The phenomenon frequently happens to families; people are usually taken as children and again and again through their adulthood into old age. Adult onset, single abduction cases are rare. It is likely the parents of any abductee were also taken, as were their children. Because of this, the phenomenon appears to grow conically into the human population.

He says the phenomenon is very common and there are probably millions of abductees worldwide.

Jacobs has found critics of his work attribute the phenomenon to about a hundred different psychological conditions. The attributions are ever changing. By contrast, the abduction reports remain very consistent over the many decades of his research.

Jacobs is not the only researcher to hear the same reports from his study subjects. Researchers from around the world are hearing the same reports of abductions and the breeding program. [180]

In 2012, Russian Prime Minister Dmitry Medvedev made some bizarre comments after a television interview when he thought the cameras had stopped rolling.

He told reporters that presidents of the country, upon taking power, would be given two top secret folders. One would be the nuclear codes and the other folder "contains information about aliens who visited our planet. Along with this, you are given a report of the absolutely secret special service that exercises control over aliens on the territory of our country.... More detailed information on this topic you can get from a well-known movie called *Men In Black....* I will not tell you how many of them are among us because it may cause panic," he said.

These comments were laughed off as if he were joking, but we believe he was serious. [69]

It is our opinion that legends of vampires come from alien abductions. Vampires come at night – they can ONLY come at night because they are burned by sunlight. Vampires are able to hypnotize and paralyze their victims, just like what happens to abductees. Genetic material is taken in the form of blood. Vampires are deathless unless they are destroyed, just like the Anunnaki. Vampires are very pale and there is a sexual mythos associated with them.

There have been reports from men who have been forced into sexual encounters with alien females. Most of the time there is no proof that these encounters took place, but there was one incident where evidence was left behind.

In the book, *Hair of the Alien,* by Bill Chalker, a 28-year-old Sydney, Australia, man, Peter Khoury, claimed that on July 23, 1992, he awoke to find two strange-looking women kneeling on his bed. While he was unable to move, he was forced into a sexual encounter. One of the women in this bizarre assault was a blonde who had very large eyes, was very pale and had sharp cheekbones and a pointy chin. The woman touched his stomach and pointed to the sky. [181]

After the encounter, Khoury found a single blond hair had been left behind. When he had the hair analyzed, it was found to be unlike any human hair type. It was completely colorless, like fishing line. The DNA results were bizarre, a strange mix of Chinese, Basque and Gaelic and also some other undetermined Asian DNA. [181]

This analysis was the first forensic evidence left behind by an alien intruder and represents physical proof that a near-human race is engaged in a hybrid breeding program.

So since they have been studying us, we think it's only fair we reciprocate.

THE ALIEN AUTOPSIES

Have you ever seen the *Alien Autopsy* program? It was released in 1995 by London-based entrepreneur Ray Santilli, who said he was given the film by a retired military cameraman who had kept some of the lower quality footage he took of an autopsy done on an alien from the 1947 Roswell crash. It was presented on television and narrated by Jonathan Frakes. [12]

The film was edited into an hour-long program. In it we see a Grey alien lying on an operating table in a room and two doctors performing an autopsy upon it.

The show depicts impressed doctors, special effects people and a major Hollywood director, who said if this is fake, we want to know who did it so we can offer them a very high-paying job in Hollywood.

The most compelling proof of at least some of the film's authenticity for us is when they slice open the skull. Wet blood is seen along the entire slice, appearing to be from thousands of real blood vessels, not from the twenty or so tubes that would have been built into the most complex automaton prop that could have been constructed at the time.

The autopsy program was released in several versions, igniting a firestorm of controversy.

A very well-researched book by Philip Mantle called *Roswell Alien Autopsy: The Truth Behind the Film That Shocked the World* (2020) presents many arguments for and against whether the film is authentic or a hoax.

Santilli continues to claim the film to be real but says that it was not in good enough condition to copy and screen. Mantle's research uncovered the fact that they used the talents of John Humphreys to create the dummies for recreating most of the autopsy footage.

Santilli insists that the original film is real and some of the footage released in the program is from the original footage and has offered a single frame of the film negative for auction.

If the film ever really existed and the dummies made by Humphreys were recreated from the images taken by a cameraman of 1947, then the creature seen in the autopsy is a humanoid described very accurately by so many abduction victims.

A small piece of the film showing the operating room before the victim is brought in was supplied to a film expert. His analysis proved the film came from 1947. The Kodak printing marks indicated the film was processed in 1927, 1947 or 1967, but the film expert's analysis of the acetate proved it came from the 1940s. It would have been impossible to have kept undeveloped film from the 1940s to use in a 1990s production.[182]

Government documents and the testimony of Col. Corso confirmed the existence of these autopsies.

WAYS THEY ARE MORE ADVANCED

If as we surmise, the Anunnaki are maintaining bases of operations here on Earth, we further surmise that they have continued to advance their technology in the long years since they first arrived.

Early stories about the Anunnaki rocketships describe fire-burning ships, or fire-breathing dragons, reminiscent of the type of rockets we use today to launch our spacecraft into space.

In more recent times, humans who encounter alien spaceships frequently suffer from radiation poisoning. It's possible they have more advanced, nuclear-driven ships now.

I was 10 years old when mankind first landed on the moon. My grandfather was sitting in the room with me watching the television coverage of Neil Armstrong placing his foot on the moon for the first time. My grandfather had tears in his eyes; it was the first and only time I ever saw that. He was born in 1900. He was alive before the lightbulb and lived to see us walk on the moon.

In order to take off from the Earth we had constructed the Saturn 5 rocket. At the time, it was the largest machine ever made by man and it held that record until the Hadron Collider was finished in 2008.

I remember being proud of mankind and impressed by our accomplishment. It sparked my lifelong love of science fiction stories.

Then I found out Buzz Aldrin had confessed that an alien ship trailed them all the way to the moon. After that I felt smaller somehow. Did the Anunnaki have a good laugh about it? Watching us nearly kill three men in a rickety, clunky spaceship? Or, were they proud of us, like parents watching a baby take a first step? Will we ever know?

We also believe that the Anunnaki and their slave races may be more spiritually advanced than we are. If the Anunnaki story is true and Sitchin's timeline is accurate, these beings were witnesses to, and the facilitators of, the beginning of our existence. We can assume the earliest religions of mankind can be sourced to the practices of the Anunnaki.

Kundalini raising and chakra stimulating can be traced back to the deep past of Tibet and Egypt. My husband and I dabbled in these practices for a few years when we were younger.

Our teachers started us with deep meditation and chakra-opening chanting. These practices are at the base of many of the world's religions and we believe the sources for these religious practices are the Anunnaki.

Those who practice chakra-opening techniques will notice over time that this expands the consciousness and facilitates abilities they didn't have before, or only had as a child.

Our teachers told us that most of the people wandering around the world are asleep, barely using 3 percent of their brain. When we are children we are more open, using about 5 percent. We have more abilities as children that we gradually lose as we grow up.

Each chakra is stimulated by the chanting of different frequencies. The Solfeggio Scale has analyzed which chakras are stimulated by which frequencies.

The crown chakra is stimulated at 963 Hz, the third eye chakra at 852 Hz, the throat chakra at 741 Hz, the heart chakra at 639 Hz, the solar plexus chakra at 528 Hz, the sacral chakra at 417 Hz and the root chakra at 396 Hz. [183] [184]

Adherents to the work of opening the chakras of the body, specifically the medullary canal of the spine, will start experiencing the abilities associated with each chakra.

For instance, the hepatic or liver chakra is vibrated using the "Fa, Ra, On," chant (at the proper frequency). When doing this chant correctly, the practitioner should feel a buzzing sensation in the spine around the level of where the liver is in the body. The ability that is stimulated by vibrating this chakra is the power of astral projection, or the ability of separating the astral body at will from the physical body. This is used by remote viewers and the reason why some people are able to separate part of their consciousness from their bodies.

Another example is the power of telepathy. The chakra for being a telepathic receiver is the solar plexus chakra and for a telepathic transmitter is the pineal or third eye chakra.

The solar plexus chakra is vibrated with the "Uo" sound and the pineal chakra is awakened with the "I (eye)" sound. Those who try vocalizing these sounds should feel a slight buzzing sensation in the middle back and the top of the head.

The heart chakra is opened with the "Om" chant, sometimes written as "AUM." The heart chakra opens the intuition. And so on. [185]

There are many books on the subject of opening Kundalini energies, and this book will not go into them in any more detail, but the point of bringing this up here is to explain that these abilities are the birthright of human beings. Anyone who has not had a serious spine-severing injury is able to do this work and open these abilities.

My husband and I can attest to this actually working. We both gained the ability to astral project and we became more and more telepathic as we continued doing the work. During this time, I regained the ability of being a human lie detector, something I could do as a child that had atrophied as I became an adult.

However, when it came to the opening of the laringeal chakra, which is the chakra of clairaudience, we decided that hearing into the astral realm was not synonymous with a life lived in twentieth century America. We both found it disconcerting to hear voices from the astral realm in our waking state. This is when we permanently left the practice. In the subsequent years, the abilities gained began to fade away.

Now, to the point of this explanation. The hybrid beings that are being bred by those who are abducting people and who have the ability to read minds, are not necessarily receiving this power from their alien DNA, but instead are maybe just doing the work necessary to open these latent abilities. They may be raised from infancy to develop and use these powers as a matter of their upbringing, which may also be further facilitated by being longer lived.

Even as a very young person learning about Jesus and the virgin Mary and the immaculate conception, I used to snort in derision, completely convinced that she was lying about being a virgin and believing that she just had some sex and got pregnant the normal way. She had a good reason to lie about how she got pregnant, since unwed pregnant girls in her society were stoned to death.

But, after researching for this book, I've become less sure about this. There are a lot of stories about women who become pregnant under mysterious circumstances who end up giving birth to extraordinary spiritual leaders.

In the Dead Sea Scrolls, there is a story about Noah's birth. His was said to have been one of these strange otherworldly births. Noah was born with many strange attributes. His skin was extra pale, almost luminescent, his hair was white and when he opened his eyes, a light came from them able to light a dark room.

Noah's father questioned the parentage of this child: "Then Lamech his father was afraid of him; and flying away came to his own father Mathusala, and said, I have begotten a son, unlike to other children. He is not human; but, resembling the offspring of the angels of heaven, is of a different nature from ours, being altogether unlike to us."

Lamech's grandfather Enoch told him to accept the baby, because he had seen that God was going to destroy the planet with a flood and that Noah was going to survive and father a new generation of man. [161]

Then there is the weird story about the first emperor of China, Qin Shi Huang, who's mother was impregnated in a rainstorm. Her husband said that as he searched for his wife who'd become separated from him, he'd seen a dragon in the sky hovering above her location.

The emperor supposedly was born with strange powers. He was credited with building many mechanical devices and created the medical practice of acupuncture because he was able to see people's acupuncture points and channels. He was associated with the creation of the Chinese calendar, writing, astronomy and mathematics.

I used to believe these kind of stories were lies told to self aggrandize prophets and other leaders, but I wonder if these stories might be evidence that the alien breeding program has been going on for thousands of years, and the children born from these encounters may actually be more spiritually advanced because of this breeding.

We believe that the perpetrators of these abductions are interested in those of us with natural ESP abilities. My husband's family is a good example. From his mother's side of the family, there is a long line of people who have ESP abilities. His mother was a prolific automatic writer who claimed to be in frequent contact with a family spirit guide named Ole Glegly.

My husband has always been very telepathic, even before doing the chakra work, and became much more so after it. Many of his family members have missing time episodes where it is possible they were victims of abduction. My husband has tried many times to break through the wall of memory block with hypnosis, but the blockages are too well placed, and he has been unable to penetrate into those memories.

For those of you who skipped the preface, my husband's brother was visited by a strange, small, floating, silver sphere at his remote forest home and also suffered from missing time issues in his early life. He once awakened to find a tall, spindly Grey alien in the doorway of his room, and another time thought he heard a cat under his bed, but when he reached down to pet it, his arm was grabbed by a hand. Directly after these incidents, he blacked out and lost time. He suffered from anxiety and other health issues through his life, rarely leaving his home until his eventual suicide in 2017.

While doing the chakra work, I enjoyed the ability to astral project and had fun with it, but my husband did not enjoy his astral projection powers. The few times he used them, he was plagued with frightening, nightmarish visions and a terrible feeling of oppression and suffocation.

Abductees frequently report emotional problems that follow them through their lives.

If these abductions and experiments are really taking place as thousands of abductees believe, it is a terrible imposition, causing a great deal of pain and terror in those who have experienced this awful violation.

It is difficult to see past the veil of their intentions concerning us. At times they seem benevolent to our species and at other times they appear vengeful and punishing.

Some people see these aliens as benevolent because they think they are trying to save us from ourselves and our own nuclear weapons. But, if what we believe is true, that they actually live here, then maybe they are just trying to save themselves. Especially if they need us and our surface-dwelling DNA. Then saving us is also saving themselves.

We think they were happy to maintain a mostly "hands off" policy in regard to us for thousands of years, but our use of nuclear weapons scared them enough that we forced them into adopting a policy of infiltration and control.

Is their breeding program for our benefit or does it suit their own purposes? In their meeting with Admiral Byrd, they as much as said that they were going to take enough of our race to ensure our survival if we destroyed ourselves with our nuclear weapons, but I don't give them credit for so much benevolence. They don't seem to care how much they damage the people they abduct. Instead I have the feeling they are serving their own needs, using us for their own purposes. If they are saving us from ourselves, we think it might be because they continue to need us to push forward with their own projects.

The alien abduction phenomenon when broken down by racial demographics shows that it is an overwhelmingly caucasian experience. About 94 percent of abductees are white. If they are protecting our species from annihilation, then why not take a more racially-balanced sampling of our population? But if, as we surmise, they are abducting people to harvest DNA for the purposes of perpetuating their own race, and if they are a caucasian branch of humanity that split away from our population thousands of years ago, then that would explain their particular interest in the DNA of white people. [186]

If this continued need of us is true, then it is similar to a parasitic, symbiotic relationship. Parasites need the host to stay alive and they are good at hiding from the host's immune system to assure their continued survival.

We think it's possible their continued breeding program may be an effort to make our two separate peoples more alike. Which may possibly facilitate the integration of our two populations and end the need for their continued secrecy.

At this point it's clear they view us as primitive savages. We think the slow release of advanced technology is an effort to close the gap between us, and the continued breeding program may be an effort to make us more civilized. But, there is evidence that their view of a civilized society is not necessarily a more diverse one.

If Professor Jacobs is right, and they are infiltrating our society in leadership roles, are we the better for it? We have witnessed some alarming changes in Earth governments in the past few decades. There has been a push towards authoritarianism. Do we see their hand in these changes? After all, it would be easier to control an authoritarian regime. You would only have to control one person instead of a congress of many.

We are seeing an expansion of white supremacy and an acceptance of it in our leaders. Are we seeing their hand here? Is it possible the Nordic "aliens," who are really the Adamic race, need whites to refrain from interbreeding with other races for a reason having to do with their breeding program? Why did they ally themselves with Hitler in World War II? Could it have something to do with keeping pure bloodlines? Does this sound like disinterested benevolence?

We know they deceive us and pretend to be visiting aliens. We think they do this to draw attention away from the fact that they are not visiting, but living here under our feet.

In the story of Valiant Thor, he claimed to have come from Venus. We now know that there is no way that Venus can support life as we know it. The environment is far too toxic. Valiant Thor appeared to be a Caucasian man with red hair. Why did he lie to us about his origins?

And, what are we to make of the sinister men in black who suppress information with threats and murders? Are we to assume this is for our own good? We think not.

There have been published authors of UFO stories who have come out later and refuted their own work. We see the hand of government suppression here. When credible UFO events occur, so often these weird men in black show up with their ridicule and discrediting procedure and when that isn't enough, their threatening and murder.

Frankly, my husband and I are worried about this ourselves. If this book hits close to the mark, we may have one of these visits ourselves. Just know this: we have written this book in good faith; this is what we really believe. If later you hear us refuting this work, you can assume there is a man in black holding a gun to our heads and forcing us to do so. If we suddenly disappear, or are killed after publishing this book, be suspicious.

REFERENCES

CHAPTER 1
HISTORY OF UFO ACTIVITY, MOSTLY IN THE UNITED STATES

1 Freedom of Information Act released National Security Agency secret report, "UFO Hypothesis and Survival Questions" (1968).

2 News report, "UFO ightings in North America jumped to nearly 6,000 in 2019," Bylvan Pereira, January 8, 2020.

3 Zoe Krasney, "What Were the Mysterious 'Foo Fighters' Sighted by WWII Night Flyers?" *Smithsonian Magazine*, August 2016.

4 Richard M. Dolan, *UFOs and the National Security State: Chronology of a Cover-up 1941-1973*. Newburyport, Massachusetts: Hampton Roads Publishing, 2002.

5 Paul Blake Smith, *M0-41: The Bombshell Before Roswell*. Kernersville, North Carolina: W&B Publishers, 2016.

6 Terrenz Sword, *The Battle of Los Angeles, 1942: The Mystery Air Raid*. New Brunswick, New Jersey: Inner Light Publications, 2003.

7 TV Channel Russia and Broadcaster Gold Media, *Foreign Agents Series*, Vitaly Pravdivtsev, writer and director, *The Third Reich: Operation UFO*, 2006. A Russian documentary based on a 1947 Soviet intelligence report about Highjump. View at youtube.com/watch?v=MwUp-PwyyvLw.

———

Roswell resources:

4 Richard M. Dolan, *UFOs and the National Security State: Chronology of a Cover-up 1941-1973*. Newburyport, Massachusetts: Hampton Roads Publishing, 2002.

8 Charles Berlitz and William L. Moore, *The Roswell Incident*. New York, New York: Grosset & Dunlap, 1980.

9 Kal K. Korff, *The Roswell UFO Crash: What They Don't Want You to Know*. New York, New York: Dell, 2000.

10 Kevin Burns, exec. prod. *Ancient Aliens,* Season 11, episode 13, "Beyond Roswell." Aired August 19, 2016, on the History Channel. Mari Johnson, dir. *Ancient Aliens,* Season 15, episode 2, "The Relics of Roswell." Aired February 1, 2020, on the History Channel.

11 Jonny Mars, dir. *UFOs: The Lost Evidence,* Season 1, episode 6, "Deathbed Confessions." Aired April 30, 2017, on AHC: Destination America.

_____

12 Tom McGough, dir. *Alien Autopsy: Fact or Fiction.* Aired August 28, 1995, on Fox Network.

13 Bob Lazar, *Dreamland: An Autobiography.* New York, New York: Interstellar, 2019.

14 Nathan Twining, "AMC Opinion Concerning 'Flying Discs," issued September 23, 1947.

_____

Project Blue Book and Majestic 12 resources:

4 Richard M. Dolan, *UFOs and the National Security State: Chronology of a Cover-up 1941-1973.* Newburyport, Massachusetts: Hampton Roads Publishing, 2002.

15 Stanton T. Friedman, *Top Secret/Majic: Operation Majestic-12 and the United States Government's UFO Cover-Up.* Boston, Massachusetts: Da Capo Press, 2005.

16 Kevin Burns, exec. prod. *Ancient Aliens,* Season 12, episode 9, "The Majestic Twelve." Aired July 7, 2017, on the History Channel.

17 Brad Steiger *Project Blue Book: The Top Secret UFO Files that Revealed a Government Cover-Up,* Red Wheel/Weiser, February 1, 2019.

18 Stanislava Turkova, executive producer, *Top Secret UFO PROJECTS declassified* series, the episode *Project Blue Book Unknown,* Netflix, 2021.

19 Wikipedia, "Project Blue Book," last modified September 6, 2022, https://en.wikipedia.org/wiki/Project_Blue_Book

_____

Kingman UFO resources:

20 Michael Pye (editor), Kirsten Dalley (editor), Stanton T. Friedman (contributor), Erich von Daniken (contributor), Nick Pope (contributor), *Exposed, Uncovered and Declassified: UFOs and Aliens: Is There Anybody Out There?* Newburyport, Massachusetts: New Page Books, June 15, 2011.

21 William Shatner, host and executive producer. *The UnXplained.* Season 2, episode 4, "The Truth About UFOS." Aired July 19, 2019, on The History Channel, .

22 Jenny Randles, *The UFO Conspiracy.* Appleton, Wisconsin: Sterling Publishing Company

Inc., 1987.

____

UFO crashes resources:

4 Richard M. Dolan, *UFOs and the National Security State: Chronology of a Cover-up 1941-1973*. Newburyport, Massachusetts: Hampton Roads Publishing, 2002.

23 Patrick Gloss, "UFOs at close sight," "UFO crashes file: Alleged UFO crashes listing," last modified March 14, 2013, ufologie.patrickgross.org/htm/crashes.htm.

24 Kevin Burns, exec. prod. *Ancient Aliens*, Season 11, episode 13, "Beyond Roswell," Aired August 19, 2016, on the History Channel.

25 Wikipedia, "Kecksburg UFO Incident," last modified August 23, 2022, https://en.wikipedia.org/wiki/Kecksburg_UFO_incident

26 Brian McGleenon, UFO cover-up claims: US hid 'another Roswell' after 1945 'avocado-shaped' crash, *Express*, June 5, 2021.

27 Don Berliner and Stanton T. Friedman, *Crash at Corona: The U.S. Military Retrieval and Cover-up of a UFO*. Los Angeles, California: Marlowe and Company, September 1, 1994.

28 Noe Torres, *Fallen Angel: UFO Crash Near Laredo, Texas*. Phoenix, Arizona: Roswell Books, September 10, 2011.

29 Imogen Braddick, "Aliens Among Us," U.S. Sun, June 15, 2021. See article at worldofthestrange.com/tag/ufo-crash.

30 Kevin D. Randle Ph.D. *When UFOs Fall From the Sky: A History of Famous Incidents, Conspiracies and Cover-Ups*. Newburyport, Massachusetts: Weiser Books, May 10, 2010.

31 "Nebraska may have had its own Roswell in 1884," The Daily Nebraskan, March 18 2007.

32 Ben Calwell, "UFO tourism gaining foothold in West Virginia county," AP News, March 2, 2019.

33 Niki D'Andrea, "Alleged UFO Crash Site at Dreamy Draw Recreation Area," *Phoenix New Times*, April 7, 2011.

34 Linda Williams, "Did a UFO crash in the valley?" Aired on Fox 10 Phoenix, January 25, 2016.

35 Historical and Preservation Society of Pottawattamie County, County Seat Council Bluffs, Iowa, *Close Encounter at Big Lake Park*, December 2007.

36 Ryan Sprague, Acast podcast series, *Somewhere in the Skies*, "The Needles UFO Crash with the UFO Bros." First aired October 18, 2020.

37 Sanya Jain, "Multiple People Report Seeing A Mysterious Blue UFO In Hawaii," NDTV report, aired January 25, 2021.

38 Nick Redfern, "A Crashed UFO in a Montana Lake?" Mysterious Universe, February 9, 2016. https://mysteriousuniverse.org/2016/02/a-crashed-ufo-in-a-montana-lake/
____

39 Wikipedia, "Mantell UFO Incident,"last modified Aug. 2, 2022, https://en.wikipedia.org/wiki/Mantell_UFO_incident.

40 "Secret Diary of Admiral Byrd," Galnet Wiki post at galnet.fandom.com/wiki/Secret_Diary_of_Admiral_Byrd.
____

Capitol incident resources:

4 Richard M. Dolan, *UFOs and the National Security State: Chronology of a Cover-up 1941-1973*. Newburyport, Massachusetts: Hampton Roads Publishing, 2002.

16 Kevin Burns, exec. prod. *Ancient Aliens*, Season 12, episode 9, "The Majestic Twelve." Aired July 7, 2017, on the History Channel.

41 Kevin D. Randle, *Invasion Washington: UFOs Over the Capitol.* New York, New York: Harper Torch, October 30, 2001.

42 Missy Sullivan, "'Flying Saucers' Over Washington Sent the Press Into a Frenzy," History.com, February 12, 2020.
____

43 Gaia Staff, "Did President Eisenhower Meet With Aliens at Holloman Air Force Base?" November 15, 2019.
____

Men in black resources:

21 William Shatner, host and executive producer, the series *The UnXplained,* episode *The Truth About UFOS,* The History Channel, July 19, 2019.

44 Nick Redfern, *The Real Men In Black: Evidence, Famous Cases, and True Stories of These Mysterious Men and their Connection to UFO Phenomena.* Weiser, June 15, 2011.
____

Mass sihtings resources:

45 Kevin Burns, exec. prod. *Ancient Aliens*, Season 6, episode 5, "Aliens in America," Aired January 31, 2014, on the History Channel.

46 Gil Carlson, *UFO Crashes, Retrievals and Government Cover-ups - Top Secret Files*, Blue Planet Project, January 1, 2016.

47 Kevin Burns, exec. prod. *Ancient Aliens*, Season 17, episode 2, "Top 10 Alien Encounters," Aired October 21, 2021, on the History Channel.

48 Wikipedia: *Japan Air Lines Cargo Flight 1628 incident*

49 Petr Vachler, *Top Secret UFO PROJECTS Declassified*, the episode, *The White House Cover-up*, Netflix, 2021.
_____

50 Petr Vachler, *Top Secret UFO PROJECTS Declassified*, the episode, *Project Blue Book Unknown*, 2021.
_____

Betty and Barney Hill resources:

22 Jenny Randles, *The UFO Conspiracy,* Sterling Publishing Company Inc., 1987.

51 Kevin Burns, exec. prod. *Ancient Aliens*, Season 14, episode 10, "Project Hybrid," Aired August 9, 2019, on the History Channel.
_____

52 David M. Jacobs, Ph.D., *The THREAT: Revealing the Secret Alien Agenda*, Simon & Schuster, March 11, 1999
_____

Travis Walton resources:

53 Travis Walton, The Walton Experience,

54 Wikipedia: *Travis Walton UFO incident*

55 Kevin Burns, exec. prod. *Ancient Aliens*, Season 4, episode 3, "The Gres," Aired February 24, 2012, on the History Channel.
_____

56 *Missing Persons by State*, World Population Reveiw, at worldpopulationreview.com/state-rankings/missing-persons-by-state.
_____

Cattle mutilations resources:

45 Kevin Burns, exec. prod. *Ancient Aliens*, Season 6, episode 5, "Aliens in America," Aired January 31, 2014, on the History Channel.

57 Wikipedia, *Cattle Mutilations.*
_____

Holloman Air Force Base meeting resources:

58 Eyes on Cinema Presents series, at youtube.com/watch?v=sq5nnrdOwqs.

59 Kevin Burns, exec. prod. *Ancient Aliens*, Season 13, episode 1, "The UFO Conspiracy," Aired April 27, 2018, on the History Channel.
———

Astroaut sightins resources:

60 Jonathan Nowzaradan, *UFOs: The Lost Evidence*, season 1, episode 13, *Pilots & Astronauts*, April 9, 2017.

61 Kevin Burns, exec. prod. *Ancient Aliens*, Season 11, episode 12, "Russia's Secret Files," Aired , August 12, 2016, on the History Channel.

62 Kevin Burns, exec. prod. *Ancient Aliens*, Season 16, episode 8, "The Space Travelers," Aired February 26, 2021, on the History Channel.
———

Alien nuclear interest resources:

22 Jenny Randles, *The UFO Conspiracy*, Sterling Publishing Company Inc., 1987.

63 Kevin Burns, exec. prod. *Ancient Aliens*, Season 14, episode 14, "The Nuclear Agenda," Aired September 6, 2019, on the History Channel.

64 Robert Lambert Hastings, *UFOs & Nukes: Extraordinary Encounters at Nuclear Weapons Sites,* Author House, January 1, 2008.

65 Emma Parry, "X-FILES Pentagon releases 1,500 pages of secret documents about shadowy UFO programme after four year battle," The Sun article, April 5, 2022.
———

66 Kevin Burns, exec. prod. *Ancient Aliens*, Season 16, episode 9, "The UFO Pioneers," Aired March 5, 2021, on the History Channel.

67 Tom DeLonge, executive producer, *Unidentified: Inside America's UFO Investigation*, May 31, 2019.

68 Kyle Mizokami, *The Weird History of Unidentified Submerged Objects*, EXONEWS, October 19, 2019.

69 Kevin Burns, exec. prod. *Ancient Aliens*, Season 11, episode 8, "The Mysterious Nine," Aired July 8, 2016, on the History Channel.

CHAPTER 2
RECENT DISCLOSURES AND A NEW GOVERNMENT POLICY

‒‒‒‒

Recent disclosures and a new government policy resources:

60 Jonathan Nowzaradan, *UFOs: The Lost Evidence*, season 1, episode 13, *Pilots & Astronauts*, April 9, 2017.

70 Matt Pearl, *Unidentified: UFOs in the Headlines*, 2021, on the History Channel.

71 Director of National Intelligence office, *Preliminary Assessment: Unidentified Aerial Phenomena*. View at dni.gov/files/ODNI/documents/assessments/Prelimary-Assessment-UAP-20210625.pdf.

CHAPTER 3
WHERE ARE THEY HIDING?

72 Stuart Clarke, executive producer, *The Alaska Triangle* series, season 1, episode 7, *The Secrets of Mount Hayes*, the Travel Channel, March 8, 2020.

73 Kevin Burns, exec. prod. *Ancient Aliens*, Season 14, episode 1, *Return to Antarctica*, Aired May 31, 2019, on the History Channel.

74 Phil Schneider, *Human-Alien Battle of 1979, Did it Happen?*, Generation Tech, https://www.youtube.com/watch?v=1wNUFv2S-2I.

75 Andrew Nock, executive producer, Ben Hansen, host, *UFO Witness series*, episode, *Aliens Underground*, Discovery+ network, February 11, 2021.

76 Stuart Clarke, executive producer, *The Alaska Triangle* series, season 2, episode 1, *The Dark Pyramid and Violent Nature*, the Travel Channel, September 10, 2021.

77 Kevin Burns, exec. prod. *Ancient Aliens*, Season 9, episode 10, *Hidden Pyramids*, Aired April 17, 2015, on the History Channel.

78 Ian O'Neill, Ph.D., *Antarctica's Spooky Cosmic Rays Might Shatter Physics As We Know It*, How Stuff Works.

79 Derek B. Fox, Steinn Sigurdsson, Sarah Shandera, Peter Mészáros, Kohta Murase, Miguel Mostafá, Stephane Coutu (Penn State University), *The ANITA Anomalous Events as Signatures of a Beyond Standard Model Particle, and Supporting Observations from IceCube*, September 25, 2018.

CHAPTER 4
MYTHS OF UNDERGROUND CIVILIZATIONS

Tuatha Dé Danann references:

80 The Highland Bard website, *The Gift of the Four Treasures* at morgynbard.com/post/the-gift-of-the-four-treasures.

81 Wikipedia: Tuatha Dé Danann.

82 Lars Bergen, *Nordic Aliens and the Fairies of Ireland: Through the Wormhole: The Tuatha Dé Danann and Celtic Irish Druids*, November 29, 2019.

83 Kevin Burns, exec. prod. *Ancient Aliens*, Season 18, episode 17, *The Shining Ones,* Aired August 19, 2022, on the History Channel.

84 Wikipedia, *Legends of Mt. Shasta*

85 Kevin Burns, exec. prod. *Ancient Aliens*, Season 17, episode 4, *The Mystery of Mount Shasta,* Aired September 17, 2021, on the History Channel.

86 JoAnne L. Huppunen, a doctor of philosophy and geophysics at Oregon State University, report, *Analysis and Interpretation of Magnetic Anomalies Observed in North Central California*, Nov. 1, 1983.

87 Kevin Burns, exec. prod. *Ancient Aliens,* Season 6, episode 11, *Aliens and Mysterious Mountains,* Aired December 13, 2013, on the History Channel.

88 An Atlas Obscura article, *Bugarach, France: Small French town or alien garage?,* November 11, 2011, at atlasobscura.com/places/bugarach.

89 Eborghi website, *Mount Mosiné: alien base and land of dark mysteries and spiritual legends,* June 27, 2020, at e-borghi.com/en/curiosities/775/mount-mosin-alien-base-and-land-of-dark-mysteries-and-spiritual-legends.html

90 Gary David article, *The Ant People of the Hopi,* October 13, 2013.

91 Gary David, *Star Shrines and Earthworks of the Desert Southwest,* Adventures Unlimited Press, October 28, 2012.

92 Kevin Burns, exec. prod. *Ancient Aliens*, Season 18, episode 20, *Secrets of Inner Earth,* Aired September 9, 2022, on the History Channel.

93 Max McClellan, producer, Lara Logan interviewer, *Sixty Minutes,* CBS news program, May 28, 2017.

94 Sarah Scoles, *Inside Robert Bigelow's Decades-Long Obsession With UFOs*, A Wired science article, February 24, 2018, at wired.com/story/inside-robert-bigelows-decades-long-obsession-with-ufos.

CHAPTER 5
THE GREAT FLOOD

95 Sir James G. Frazer, *The Great Flood: A Handbook of World Flood Myths,* originally published in 1743.
_____

Flood myth resources:

96 The Bible, The Old Testament, *Genesis.*

97 Wikipedia.com, Flood Myth, Great Flood (China), Unu Pachakuti, List of Flood Myths, Mesoamerican Flood Myths, Ragnarok, Namu Doryeong.

98 Kevin Burns, exec. prod. *Ancient Aliens,* Season 9, episode 8, *The Great Flood,* Aired December 23, 2014, on the History Channel.

99 Ignacioua L. Donnelly, Atlantis, the Antediluvian World, Dover Publications, December 8, 2011.

CHAPTER 6
A SMALL EXTINCTION EVENT

100 Johán B. Kloosterman's manifesto on Hijszeler's discovery, *The Usselo Horizon, a Worldwide Charcoal-Rich Layer of Alleröd Age,* presented to the *New Scenarios of Solar System Evolution,* symposium at the University of Bergamo, June of 1999.

101 Laura Geggel, *10 extinct giants that once roamed North America,* Live Science article, August 15, 2015, at livescience.com/51793-extinct-ice-age-megafauna.html.

102 D. J. Kennett, J. P. Kennett, A. West, C. Mercer, S S. Que Heel. L Bement, T. E. Bunch, M. Sellers and W. S. Wolbach, *Nanodiamonds in the Younger Dryas Boundary Sediment Layer,* Journal of Geology study, January 2, 2009.

103 Charles R. Kinzie, Shane S. Que Hee, Adrienne Stich, Kevin A. Tague, Chris Mercer, Joshua J. Razink, Douglas J. Kennett, Paul S. DeCarli, Ted E. Bunch, James H. Wittke, Isabel Israde-Alcántara, James L. Bischoff, Albert C. Goodyear, Kenneth B. Tankersley, David R. Kimbel, Brendan J. Culleton, Jon M. Erlandson, Thomas W. Stafford, Johan B. Kloosterman, Andrew M. T. Moore, Richard B. Firestone, J. E. Aura Tortosa, J. F. Jordá Pardo, Allen West, James P. Kennett and Wendy S. Wolbach, *Nanodiamond-Rich Layer across Three Continents Consistent with Major Cosmic Impact at 12,800 Cal BP,* Journal of Geology study, September 2014.

104 Julie Cohen, *Study examines 13,000-year-old nanodiamonds from multiple locations across three continents,* University of California at Santa Barbara, a paper published in 2014

105 *Paleoindian Database of the Americas,* PIDBA, at pidba.utk.edu.

106 David Anderson, Albert C. Goodyear, Thomas W. Stafford Jr. and James P. Kennett, *Human Population Decline in North America during the Younger Dryas,* in a Research Gate publication, December 2009, at researchgate.net/publication/241587194_Human_Population_Decline_in_North_America_during_the_Younger_Dryas.

CHAPTER 7
HIAWATHA IS FOUND

107 Paul Voosen, *Massive crater under Greenland's ice points to climate-altering impact in the time of humans: The 31-kilometer-wide Hiawatha crater may have formed as recently as 12,800 years ago when a 1.5-kilometer asteroid struck Earth,* November 14, 2018.

108 Kurt Kjær and 21 co-authors, *A large impact crater beneath Hiawatha Glacier in northwest Greenland,* report in Science Advances, 2018.

109 K. Wünnemann and R. Weiss, *Philosophical Transactions of the Royal Society A: Mathematical, Physical and Engineering Sciences,* review article, October 28, 2015, at royalsociety-publishing.org/doi/10.1098/rsta.2014.0381.

110 William Bramley, *The Gods of Eden,* William Heinemann, 1995.

111 Graham Hancock, *Fingerprints of the Gods,* Dahlin Family Press, 1989.

112 William Shatner, host and executive producer. *The UnXplained.* Season 2, episode 4, "The Underground World." Aired August 8, 2020, on The History Channel.

113 Kevin Burns, exec. prod. *Ancient Aliens,* Season 2, episode 8, *Unexplained Structures,* Aired December 16, 2010, on the History Channel.

114 Kevin Burns, exec. prod. *Ancient Aliens,* Season 12, episode 16, *Return to Gobekli Tepe,* Aired September 15, 2017, on the History Channel.

CHAPTER 8
HOW MANY TIMES HAS IT HAPPENED?

115 Space.com website at space.com/10-earth-impact-craters-you-should-visit.

116 Wikipedia, "Impact Events," last modified September 9, 2022, https://en.wikipedia.org/wiki/Impact_event

117 The Planetary and Space Science Centre (PASSC) at passc.net/AboutUs/index.html. Earth Impact Database: passc.net/EarthImpactDatabase/New%20website_05-2018/Index.html.

118 Laura Geggel, "Atlantis Found (Again)! And Exasperated Scientists (Again) Raise Their Eyebrows," Live Science, November 28, 2018

119 Wikipedia, "Charles Hapgood," last modified August 31, 2022, https://en.wikipedia.org/wiki/Charles_Hapgood

CHAPTER 9
MEET THE TETHANS

120 Dr. Michael E. Salla, *Antarctica's Hidden History*, Exopolitics Consultants, March 25, 2018.

CHAPTER 10
SO MANY IMPOSSIBLE THINGS

121 Kevin Burns, exec. prod. *Ancient Aliens*, Season 12, episode 4, *The Alien Architects*, Aired May 19, 2017, on the History Channel.

122 Eric Betz, "Is Caral, Peru, the Oldest City in the Americas? *Discover Magazine*, December 23, 2020. https://www.discovermagazine.com/the-sciences/is-caral-peru-the-oldest-city-in-the-americas.

123 Kevin Burns, exec. prod. *Ancient Aliens*, season 18, episode 3, *Beneath the Sacred Temples*, Aired January 21, 2022, on the History Channel.

124 Kevin Burns, exec. prod. *Ancient Aliens*, season 1, episode 1, *The Evidence*, Aired April 20, 2010, on the History Channel.

125 Erik J. Marsh, "Arthur Posnansky, the Czar of Tiwanaku Archaeology," *Archaeology Bulletin* March 2019.

126 Wikipedia, "Sacsayhuamán," last modified May 20, 2022, https://en.wikipedia.org/wiki/Sacsayhuam%C3%A1n

127 Kevin Burns, exec. prod. *Ancient Aliens*, season 17, episode 1, *The Lost City of Peru*, Aired August 6, 2021, on the History Channel.

128 Kevin Burns, exec. prod. *Ancient Aliens*, season 12, episode 7, *The City of the Gods*, Aired June 9, 2017, on the History Channel.

129 Jonathan Nowzaradan, *UFOs: The Lost Evidence*, season 1, episode 13, *Ancient UFO Earth Landings*, April 16, 2017.

130 Wikipedia, "Olmecs," last modified Sept. 20, 2022, https://en.wikipedia.org/wiki/Olmecs.

131 Kevin Burns, exec. prod. *Ancient Aliens*, season 15, episode 1, *The Mystery of Nan Madol*, Aired January 25, 2020, on the History Channel.

132 Wikipedia, "Baalbek Stones," last modified August 29, 2022, https://en.wikipedia.org/wiki/Baalbek_Stones.

133 Veda Vyasa and Valmiki Adi-Kavi, *Mahabharata and Ramayana: The Epics of India.* Translated by Romesh C. Dutt, 2015.

134 Wikipedia, "Dvārakā," last modified September 2, 2022, https://en.wikipedia.org/wiki/Dv%C4%81rak%C4%81

135 Kevin Burns, exec. prod. *Ancient Aliens*, season 15, episode 6, *The World Before Time*, Aired February 29, 2020, on the History Channel.

CHAPTER 11
MAINSTREAM ACADEMIA AND THE PSEUDOSCIENTISTS

136 Scott Creighton, *The Great Pyramid Hoax: The Conspiracy to Conceal the True History of Ancient Egypt,"* Bear and Company, December 15, 2016.

137 Zecharia Sitchin, book 1 of *The Earth Chronicles,* series, *The 12th Planet*, Harper, March 27, 2007.

138 John Anthony West and Robert Schoch, *Sphinx water erosion hypothesis,* paper on Wikipedia, 1992.

139 Christopher Dunn, *The Giza Power Plant: Technologies of Ancient Egypt.* Rochester, Vermont: Bear and Company, August 1, 1998.

140 Professor Paul Micallef, *Mnajdra Prehistoric Temple A Calendar in Stone,* S.N., 1989.

141 Kevin Burns, exec. prod. *Ancient Aliens*, season 16, episode 4, *Giants of the Mediterranean,* Aired December 11, 2020, on the History Channel.

142 Kevin Burns, exec. prod. *Ancient Aliens*, season 13, episode 8, *Island of the Giants*, Aired July 27, 2018, on the History Channel.

143 Mark Carlotto, Ph.D., *Before Atlantis: New Evidence of a Previous Technological Civilization.* CreateSpace, October 3, 2018.

CHAPTER 12
INEXPLICABLE ANCIENT SUMERIAN KNOWLEDGE

144 Wikipedia," Library of Ashurbanipal," last modified June 20, 2022, https://en.wikipedia. org/wiki/Library_of_Ashurbanipal.

CHAPTER 13
THE BABYLONIAN CREATION MYTH

145 Kerry Lotzov, "How Did the Moon Form: Museum Planetary Science Researcher Prof. Sara Russell Explains the Origins of Earth's Closest Companion," Natural History Museum article.

CHAPTER 14
FOLLOW THE SUPPRESSION

146 Wikipedia, "Nordic Aliens," last modified July 26, 2022, https://en.wikipedia.org/wiki/ Nordic_aliens.

147 Legends of America website, "Giant skeletons in Virginia," legendsofamerica.com/giants-west-virginia.

148 Richard |. Dewhurst, *The Ancient Giants Who Ruled America: The Missing Skeletons and the Great Smithsonian Cover-Up.* Hopewell, New Jersey: Bear and Company, December 27, 2013.

149 Jason Colavito, "Newspaper Accounts of Giants," website at https://www.jasoncolavito. com/newspaper-accounts-of-giants.html

150 "Stone Age in Connecticut: Two Complete Skeletons of Great Antiquity Dug Up by Prof. Moorehead," *New York Times*, August 19, 1922.

151 Historical Happenings and Oddities website at cynthiaripleymiller.wordpress. com/2013/05/26/are-giants-real.

152 "Strange Skeletons Found: Indications That Tribe Hitherto Unknown Once Lived in Wisconsin," *New York Times*, May 4, 1912.

153 Richard E. Daggett, *Julio C. Tello, Politics and Peruvian Archaeology,* University of Maine Department of Anthropology, December 17, 2016.

154 Vittorio Di Cesare and Adriano Forgione, Malta: Skulls of the Mother Goddess, article, bibliotecapleyades.net/esp_maltaskulls_1.htm

155 Melanie Drury, "Why are these elongated skulls at Hal Saflieni Hypogeum shrouded in mystery?" Guideme Malta, March 2021, at guidememalta.com/en/why-are-these-elongated-skulls-at-hal-saflieni-hypogeum-shrouded-in-mystery.

156 "Malta Caves, missing children, strange animals," Above Top Secret at https://www.above-topsecret.com/forum/thread216479/pg1

157 Rena, "This Prehistoric Underground Temple Hides The Unexplained Mystery Of Elongated Skulls," April 14, 2015, at humansbefree.com/2015/04/this-prehistoric-underground-temple-hides-the-unexplained-mystery-of-elongated-skulls.html.

158 "Baronmaya, Ecuador shows the Skeletons of an Ancient Race of Giant Humans," Cosmos Chronicle at cosmoschronicle.com/ecuador-present-the-skeletons-of-an-ancient-race-of-giant-humans.

159 Andrew Curry, "Here Are the Ancient Sites ISIS Has Damaged and Destroyed," *National Geographic*, September 1, 2015, at nationalgeographic.com/history/article/150901-isis-destruction-looting-ancient-sites-iraq-syria-archaeology.

160 Wikipedia, "Destruction of cultural heritage by the Islamic State," last modified August 24, 2022, https://en.wikipedia.org/wiki/Destruction_of_cultural_heritage_by_the_Islamic_State.

161 Kevin Burns, exec. prod. *Ancient Aliens*, season 7, episode 8, *Alien Breeders*, Aired May 14, 2014, on the History Channel.

CHAPTER 15
WHAT DO ANCIENT SUMERIAN GODS HAVE TO DO WITH ALIENS?

162 Gerald Clark, *The Anunnaki of Nibiru: Mankind's Forgotten Creators, Enslavers, Destroyers, Saviors and Hidden Architects of the New World Order,* CreateSpace, August 4, 2013.

163 Thomas O'Toole, "Orbiting Eye Reveals Mystery Space Monster," *Washington Post,* December 30, 1983. Article can now be found on The Rabbit Hole website at rabbithole2.com/presentation/news/cosmic_news/orbiting_eye_reveals_mystery_space_monster.htm.

164 "Does the Sun Have a Dark Companion?" *Newsweek,* June 28, 1982. Excerpt can be viewed at The Rabbit Hole website at rabbithole2.com/presentation/news/cosmic_news/does_the_sun_have_a_dark_companion.htm.

165 Peter Tompkins and Hugh Harleston Jr., *Mysteries of the Mexican Pyramids,* New York, New York: Harper Collins, March 31, 1987.

166 Zecharia Sitchin, author, Janet Sitchin, editor, *The Anunnaki Chronicles.* Hopewell, New Jersey: Bear and Company, September 28, 2015.

167 Zecharia Sitchin, *The Lost Book of Enki: Memoirs and Prophecies of an Extraterrestrial*

God. Hopewell, New Jersey: Bear and Company, August 16, 2004.

168 Zecharia Sitchin, *Genesis Revisited.* New York, New York: Avon October 1, 1990.

169 Micheal A. Cremo and Richard L. Thompson, *Forbidden Archeology: The Hidden History of the Human Race.* Los Angeles, California: Bhaktivedanta Book Publishing, January 1, 1998.

170 Stephanie Dalley, translator, *Oxford World Classics*, book series, *Myths From Mesopotamia: Creation, the Flood, Gilgamesh and Others*, OUP Oxford, 1989.

171 Howard Hughes Medical Institute, "Evidence That Human Brain Evolution Was A Special Event," *Science News*, January 12, 2005.

172 Simon Neubauer, Jean-Jacques Hublin and Philipp Gunz, "The evolution of modern human brain shape," January 24, 2018, science.org/doi/full/10.1126/sciadv.aao5961.

173 Rajatkumar Dani, "Researchers find proof of ancient 'atomic war' a great many years prior," *Times of India,* March 22, 2019.

174 Zecharia Sitchin, book 3 of *The Earth Chronicles*, series, *The Wars of Gods and Men*. New York, New York: Harper, March 27, 2007.

175 Andre Parrot, *Sumer: The Dawn of Art.* Golden Press, January 1, 1961.

176 Wikipedia, "Magnetic field of Mars," last modified September 15, 2022, at en.wikipedia.org/wiki/Magnetic_field_of_Mars.

177 European Space Agency, "Cydonia - the face on Mars," September 21, 2006.

178 John E. Brandenburg, *Death on Mars: The Discovery of a Planetary Nuclear Massacre*, Adventures Unlimited Press book, February 10, 2015, and Evidence for a Large Anomalous Nuclear Explosions in Mars Past, article at hou.usra.edu/meetings/lpsc2015/eposter/2660.pdf.

CHAPTER 16
THE CONTINUED BREEDING PROGRAM

179 Prof. David M. Jacobs, *Walking Among Us: The Alien Plan to Control Humanity.* New York, New York: Disinformation Books, September 1, 2015

180 David M. Jacobs, *The THREAT: Revealing the Secret Alien Agenda.* New York, New York: Simon and Schuster, March 11, 1999.

181 Bill Chalker, *Hair of the Alien: DNA and Other Forensic Evidence of Alien Abductions.* New York, New York: Gallery Books, July 19, 2005.

182 Philip Mantle, *Roswell Alien Autopsy: The Truth Behind the Film That Shocked the World,*

originally published by Roswell Books in 2012, then published by Flying Disk Press in 2017 with a revised edition in 2020. Our source is the 2020 edition.

183 *Solfeggio Scale – The Ultimate Guide*, attuned vibrations website at attunedvibrations.com/solfeggio-scale.

184 Jack Roberts and Michael Light, *The Secrets of Solfeggio Frequencies*, January 12, 2018.

185 Genevieve Lewis Paulson, *Kundalini and the Chakras: Evolution in This Lifetime: A Practical Guide.* Woodbury, Minnesota: Llewellyn Worldwide, September 8, 2002.

186 Stephanie Kelley-Romano, *A Report on the Demographics and Beliefs of Alien Abduction Experiencers,* Bates College, January 2006, at *researchgate.net/publication/333634035_A_Report_on_the_Demographics_and_Beliefs_of_Alien_Abduction_Experiencers.*

INDEX

ABOUT THE AUTHORS

LESLIE SHAW

Leslie Shaw was born in downtown Los Angeles in 1959. She has been writing, drawing and painting since childhood.

She attended El Camino College part time for a few years. She majored in fine art with a minor in art history, including ancient art history studies.

She transferred to the prestigious California Institute of the Arts. She graduated from CAL ARTS with a bachelor's degree in experimental animation.

Leslie worked in motion control camera effects for movies and television for five years, then in television for nine years doing computer animation.

After moving to the high desert she began doing computer graphics for the Hi-Desert Star and then moved into the editorial department where she worked as a journalist and paginator for 17 years. She is now semi-retired but still works for the newspaper part time.

Leslie is a lifelong science fiction fan, and is very well read in this genre. Throughout her life, she has had a keen interest in ufology and has spent many years of reading and research in this field.

She has written news articles, poetry and has now completed her first book, "Who They Are, and What They're Up To," in which she expounds on her theories about UFOs and the beings who are flying them.

She and her husband Stephen now reside in Desert Hot Springs in Southern California.

STEPHEN SHAW

Stephen's education began at the Montessori School. He developed a proclivity for languages, music, math and the sciences. Stephen writes, records and performs classical and jazz music. He served six years in the US Navy. He worked with his father as a cabinetmaker and builder while putting himself through medical school. He was a state-licensed practitioner of Chinese medicine and acupuncture for 20 years and a teacher of the Yang and Chen styles of Tai Chi Chuan for 23 years.

Stephen studied geology in college and is a life-long rock hound.

He wrote the content for a website detailing methods using homeopathy and Chinese medicine as adjacent treatments for cancer.

Stephen's family has a long, multi-generational history of strange, other-worldly phenomena. For more on this, read the Preface.

Made in the USA
Monee, IL
02 June 2023

34975664R00154